BROTHER
ROBERT

BROTHER ROBERT

Growing Up with Robert Johnson

ANNYE C. ANDERSON
WITH PRESTON LAUTERBACH
FOREWORD BY ELIJAH WALD

New York

Hachette Books
Hachette Book Group
1290 Avenue of the Americas
New York, NY 10104
HachetteBooks.com
Twitter.com/HachetteBooks
Instagram.com/HachetteBooks

First Edition: June 2020

Published by Hachette Books, an imprint of Perseus Books, LLC,
a subsidiary of Hachette Book Group, Inc. The Hachette Books
name and logo is a trademark of the Hachette Book Group.

The Hachette Speakers Bureau provides a wide range of authors for speaking events.
To find out more, go to www.hachettespeakersbureau.com or call (866) 376-6591.

The publisher is not responsible for websites (or their
content) that are not owned by the publisher.

Reveal photo on page 151 is courtesy of the author's collection.

Print book interior design by Amy Quinn

Library of Congress Cataloging-in-Publication Data
Names: Anderson, Annye C. author. | Lauterbach, Preston, author.
Title: Brother Robert : growing up with Robert Johnson / by Mrs. Annye C.
Anderson with Preston Lauterbach.
Description: First edition. | New York : Hachette Books, 2020. | Includes
index.
Identifiers: LCCN 2019034235 | ISBN 9780306845260 (hardcover) | ISBN
9780306845277 (epub)
Subjects: LCSH: Johnson, Robert, 1911–1938. | Blues musicians—United
States—Biography. | Johnson, Robert, 1911–1938—Family. | Anderson,
Annye C.
Classification: LCC ML420.J735 A75 2020 | DDC 782.421643092 [B]—dc23
LC record available at https://lccn.loc.gov/2019034235

ISBNs: 978-0-306-84526-0 (hardcover), 978-0-306-84527-7 (ebook)

Printed in the United States of America

LSC-C

10 9 8 7 6 5 4 3 2

This book is dedicated to the memory of my daughter Hughia, who believed my story is just as important as Robert Johnson's. Also to Sister Carrie, who suffered greatly and who never got her reward.

CONTENTS

Contents

FOREWORD BY ELIJAH WALD

When we listen to a favorite artist, they often seem to understand us better than we know ourselves. As we keep listening in different situations, through our changing lives, we inevitably come to feel we know them in similarly deep ways. Robert Johnson's recordings have a particular intimacy because no other musicians are involved. We are alone with just his voice and guitar, hearing his breath between phrases, the strain in his high notes, the rattle of his slide on the frets, and the occasional murmured comments, as if he were talking directly to us.

For more than eighty years, the only way to experience Robert Johnson has been through those recordings. For millions of people all around the world, he *is* those recordings. We have listened to them over and over, spent hours, days, and years with them. So it is easy to feel we have spent that time with Johnson, and to forget that he only spent a few days making them and what we are hearing is barely an hour and a half of his life.

Annye Anderson really did spend days and weeks with Robert Johnson, over many years, not as a disembodied voice but as a tall, lanky, handsome, warm, and exciting older brother. She was a little girl and her memories of him are a little girl's memories. If you ask her about his travels or romantic relationships, about juke joints and rent parties, or about the pleasures and dangers of his life on the road, she tends to say she didn't know about that part of his life. She knew him when he was staying at her daddy's house in Memphis, or nearby at their sister Carrie's. For the rest, she'll say, "I didn't have him in my pocket."

The first memory of Robert Johnson in this book is of a long-legged eighteen-year-old carrying a toddler up a flight of stairs. The last is of him playing at a party celebrating Joe Louis's victory over Max Schmeling. In between are memories of him taking a little girl to the movies, caring for her father's horse, teaching her a simple piece on the piano, and sitting outside with his guitar, singing nursery rhymes for her and her friends or playing upbeat tunes that got them dancing.

Annye Anderson's Brother Robert was not the rambling, blues-singing loner a lot of us have imagined; he was part of a bustling, vibrant household and neighborhood. His musical skills made him distinctive, but their older brother Son was also an exceptional musician and often teamed up with him as a musical duo and for hoboing journeys. They played blues, including songs we know from the records, but also lots of other music. When you ask Mrs. Anderson about their repertoire, she says Johnson would play whatever people wanted to hear: "I remember him asking all the guests, and even the children, 'What's your pleasure?'" Maybe late in the evening they wanted to hear a moody blues like "Come On In My Kitchen." Maybe they wanted Son to liven up the mood with a Fats Waller number. Maybe they wanted to hear about rambling and hoboing, and the two men would harmonize and yodel on Jimmie Rodgers's "Waiting for a Train." Or maybe it was Annye's turn to show off and they'd back her on a song-and-dance routine from the new Ginger Rogers musical.

Johnson is at the center of this book, but he is surrounded by a lot of other people. One striking figure is Charles Dodds, who became Charles Spencer after a lynch mob forced him to move to Memphis. A barber, carpenter, and jack of all trades, he also seems to have been a formidable musician and mentored the young Johnson—the son of his first wife by another man, but welcomed as a son to the Memphis household—along with a changing cast of children, grandchildren, wives, ex-wives, and their various spouses and partners.

Another notable character is Sister Carrie. In the first half of the book she is the "fly" member of the family, the one with a radio and a phonograph, whose home was Johnson's favored stopping place when he came back through Memphis in later years as a working musician. In the second half she is the one who keeps the family connected as they move north, takes care of the ones who need care—and then, when Johnson's music is discovered by a new generation of fans around the world, becomes tangled in the increasingly complicated strands of his legacy.

Finally, there is the voice that tells the stories. I would have enjoyed this book under any circumstances but particularly appreciate it because it gave me the opportunity to meet Annye Anderson. Preston Lauterbach invited Peter Guralnick and me to spend an afternoon with them, and we planned to ask her some questions about Robert Johnson and Memphis. Before we could get to that she was discussing her plans to travel when the book comes out: first to England, then South Africa and France. The mention of France reminded her of her friend Archie Shepp, the avant-garde jazz saxophonist, and soon she was talking about Max Roach and Julius Lester, likewise friends in her current hometown of Amherst, Massachusetts. Then the conversation moved to her barbecue sauce, which she has marketed to merchants around the state, and to her husband's laboratory work and meeting Dr. Charles Drew, the African American surgeon who pioneered modern blood banks. Listening to her plans, enthusiasm, and range of interests at age ninety-three, I can only imagine how vibrant and fascinating she must have been as a young woman. And I cannot help thinking about all the stories we will never know—in particular all the African American stories—because they never happened to intersect with a blues legend.

Robert Johnson's music is timeless and speaks to us today in ways nobody could have imagined in the 1930s. But it was also the music of a particular time and place, and to some extent of a particular family. He spent time in the Mississippi Delta and further south in Hazlehurst, traveled west to Texas, north to Chicago, and east to New York. His musical influences included Son House and Willie Brown at back-country picnics; Leroy Carr, Kokomo Arnold, and Lonnie Johnson on wind-up Victrolas; Jimmie Rodgers on the radio; Gene Autry in the movies; and whatever was hitting on jukeboxes wherever he traveled.

Memphis was one of many places Johnson stayed and played—but it was a special place for him. His mother, Julia, first left him with Charles Spencer when he was seven years old, and that remained the closest thing he had to a permanent home. He joined his mother for a few years in the rural Delta, briefly married and tried to settle on a farm, and stayed with lots of other people in other places. But he never set down roots anywhere else, and till the end of his life he kept coming back to Memphis and the Spencers.

I first read this manuscript hoping to learn more about Robert Johnson, and it was interesting to read Mrs. Anderson's recollections of the people who raised and nurtured him: Charles Spencer, the closest he ever knew to a father; Son, his half-brother and musical partner; and his half-sister Carrie, who seems to have been something like a second mother to him. As I kept reading, I began to picture Johnson in a new way, as part of that big, complicated, talented household. I see the house, with the barber chair in the front room. I imagine him coming through the door and little Annye jumping up and down with excitement, Sister Carrie telling her to calm down and run an errand while she runs him a bath. I see him in a Stetson hat standing by the piano, strumming along as Brother Son sings the latest Louis Armstrong hit, or relaxing next to the radio with his stepfather, enjoying the Grand Ole Opry.

Obviously that picture is a mix of Mrs. Anderson's memories and my imagination, but it makes me hear Johnson's records in a different way. I had always pictured him in the Delta or on the road. I could hear the modern touches in his music, his debt to urban blues stars like Carr and Peetie Wheatstraw and the brilliant way he blended their contemporary sound with the rough power and rhythmic sophistication of the older Delta players—but I imagined him in rural Mississippi, impressing the other young players around Clarksdale with what he'd picked up from records and the road. That is the picture we get from people like his sometime partners Johnny Shines and Robert Lockwood Jr., and admiring contemporaries like McKinley Morganfield, a Delta field hand who would soon move up to Chicago and become famous as Muddy Waters.

Johnson certainly spent time around the Delta in his later years, so that picture isn't wrong. But his records sound different when I imagine him standing by the piano in Carrie's house playing the Scrapper Blackwell guitar licks as Son matches Carr's mellow tenor and understated piano on "Blues Before Sunrise." Or the two of them walking to Beale Street and busking in Handy Park, playing whatever suited the urban passersby, and maybe getting invited up to a room in the Peabody to play a mix of pop hits and down-home field music for some rich white folks. Thinking of Johnson as a hip, urban musician spicing his music with Delta touches rather than a Delta musician picking up on the latest urban sounds doesn't make his records sound better or worse—but it adds another layer and changes the way I hear his musical choices.

I am also reminded of all the music we can never hear. I want to know how Son sounded when he did his Louis Armstrong imitations, and how Johnson played on those numbers: did he strum swing chords, like he does in his intro to "They're Red Hot," or pick an intricate solo in the style of Lonnie Johnson—or did he play something of his own that I can't imagine? Was he always the center of attention, or did he sometimes sit back with the rest of the family and enjoy the show? I want to know more about Son, and about Charles Dodds Spencer, who knew his way around a half-dozen instruments but had quit playing by the time Mrs. Anderson was born. And I wish I could see Mrs. Anderson herself at age twelve, trucking across the stage of the Palace Theater, and hear the orchestra playing their Memphis variant of the latest Count Basie hits.

The great pleasure of this book is the way it expands that world, adding small touches that bring it to life. The older generation included Mrs. Anderson's mother, Mollie Spencer, who had come up from Mississippi and "used to eat her greens and her hot water cornbread with her hands, like the Africans," and Johnson's mother,

Julia, who insisted on doing her washing outside on a "rub board" rather than using sister Carrie's washing machine. The younger generation included Mrs. Anderson's husband, who played with Jimmie Lunceford, then worked as a chemist in Washington and Boston; and her sister Charlyne, who was "always a bookworm, reading, reading, reading," studied Latin, and became their high school valedictorian.

Less pleasurable are the stories of what happened after Johnson's records were reissued and he became the most famous name in early blues. Reading Mrs. Anderson's version I'm struck by how very few of these stories have been told by African Americans who were directly involved. Virtually the entire history of the "blues revival" has been written by white fans and even the most sympathetic are writing from outside that culture, while many have been involved in the sorts of theft and appropriation that Mrs. Anderson details with eloquent anger.

There is much more to be said about all of that, but it's time for me to get out of the way. I came to this project hoping to learn more about Robert Johnson and ended up learning about a lot of other people, including an extraordinary nonagenarian who has been quiet long enough. I am forever grateful that before moving on she decided to have her say.

Introducing
Mrs. Annye C. Anderson

By Preston Lauterbach

In April of 2018, I heard from my agent that a relative of Robert Johnson wanted me to write her book—Annye C. Anderson. Her name rang a distant bell. Still, folks had wanted me to write their life stories before, and I hadn't done one of those yet.

I called her up. Her voice almost instantly assured me that this book needed to happen. She sounds unmistakably, beautifully Southern. Clear, though. She told me she'd soon turn ninety-two. The voice sounded vital. I never doubted that she is who she claims to be, "Baby Sis" to Robert Johnson. The voice settled that. After all, they learned to speak from some of the same people.

She told me that she's not a first-name person. I would refer to her as Mrs. Anderson, and she to me as Mr. Lauterbach. I offered to go and meet her.

Mrs. Anderson did not invite me inside of her home on that first visit. I picked her up outside of her place. She wore a turban, as she often does. I folded up her walker and stuck it in the trunk of my car. We headed into town. She gets out just about every day, and is known on the streets. She told me she disguises herself as a bag lady so that nobody will knock her over the head. With her bag-lady disguise and insistence on using titles, Mrs. Anderson is both familiar and formal.

She'd found us a place to sit and talk, at a workspace in a former bank. The guy who ran it gave her the space for free, so he stuck us in what must have been a phone booth near around the time Mrs. Anderson was born. As we discussed how to collaborate on her book, Mrs. Anderson made it clear that she wouldn't be doing any typing. I'd interview her, transcribe her words to the page, put the story in proper order, and give it to her to fix the way she liked. We figured we'd start right away.

Mrs. Anderson made the point, early and often, that family has been marginalized in Robert Johnson's story. I believe that, and I think the fact that Mrs. Anderson has come forward at this late date seems all the more surprising and exciting because of that discrepancy. I don't think that many Robert Johnson fans are aware that a person this close to the mythical man still lives among us.

I've been around historical figures who've exaggerated their roles or expertise, but I never felt skeptical towards her. I wish I had a nickel for every time I asked Mrs. Anderson what I thought would be the crucial Robert

Johnson question only to hear, "Honey, I didn't have him in my pocket." Mrs. Anderson was twelve when Robert Johnson died, and even though she has a strong memory, she says that she and Robert lived different lives. As much as her memories tell us about Robert Johnson, more so, they illustrate what he saw, whom he spoke with, and what was discussed—precious gritty little details of life.

One aspect of Robert Johnson's way of thinking that stood out to me, listening to her, is how he compartmentalized. He kept his road life quiet around his family, and he kept his family life quiet on the road. He came from a complicated background, like history torn from the pages of William Faulkner, an innocent child born of violence and adultery. His secretiveness about his different lives reminds me of how children of divorced parents learn to avoid talking about mom's family in front of dad and vice versa. Until now, fans have mostly had the recollections of Robert Johnson's traveling buddies, and so, only that side of him. Mrs. Anderson knew Johnson as few people ever did, and certainly as no one else living does. She brings us that other side.

On the second day of our collaboration, we met at the workspace, but this time got sent to "the vault," a large conference room. I set out my tape recorder, notepad, and computer on a rectangular table. Mrs. Anderson tottered in wearing the bag-lady disguise. A number of plastic drugstore sacks hung from the handles of her walker.

I had my recorder rolling for our interview, and on the playback, can hear my voice tighten as I react to seeing what she carried in those plastic bags. First, she handed me a sheaf of family death certificates and marriage licenses, which I looked through and made notes from. Next came a pile of photographs, showing her father, Robert's mother. Finally, she removed a little box that had once carried a bottle of sewing machine oil back in the 1930s, the kind Mrs. Anderson had picked up on errands for her sister, a seamstress. "This is the highlight," she said. "This photo has never been out."

I remember the air thinning and my heart beating rubbery. But there's something soothing about Mrs. Anderson's dignity, and I sound composed as I look into the little blue box, saying, "If you put this on the cover of your book, it'll help sales tremendously."

She picked more items out of the shopping bags and placed them in front of me. On the recording, you can practically hear the lump fill my throat and the tears brim in my eyes, as I say, "that's worth a million dollars."

After that day at the office, I went back to my properly shabby motel room, and, sipping on a cold beer, noticed the date, May 8—Robert Johnson's birthday.

Mrs. Anderson sent me home with a jar of her home-made barbecue sauce. "It's high end," she said. "All organic." For a label, she'd stuck a nametag to the jar that read HELLO MY NAME IS: Mizz Annye.

Our next meeting took place in Memphis on the eightieth anniversary of Robert Johnson's death, August 16, 2018. We stood and talked in the overgrown yard of the abandoned house where they used to live. We looked around at the spots where he used to sit and pick his guitar. The mosquitoes got fierce and we fled for the air-conditioned car to continue her reminiscence.

We were sitting in the car on her old street when a couple of guys walked up to her window. They asked in a not unfriendly way who we were and what we were up to. Mrs. Anderson gave them a fake name. When they wandered off, she told me one of her pet phrases. "If everything somebody says to me ends in a question mark, they can forget it." I told her that put me in a strange position, and she replied with another one of her favorites. "No honey, I'm on your time."

We drove down a main avenue of South Memphis and saw a massive mural of Robert Johnson painted on the side of a brick building in a vacant parking lot. We stopped to look, and asked a guy to take our picture in front of the mural. He said he knew who the man with the guitar was, he had just watched *O Brother, Where Art Thou?*

Mrs. Anderson hasn't reached the age of ninety-three by worrying about what she eats. In Memphis, we went out for fried catfish, fried green tomatoes, and fried chicken, sometimes at the same meal. For something un-fried, we had pork barbecue. At the Blue and White Diner in Tunica, Mississippi, the bill came to $32.20. I flashed the receipt to Mrs. Anderson and she laughed.

She remembers a time in Memphis when only African Americans cooked barbecue, and the craze hadn't yet swept the city. Three barbecue kings in particular stood out—Johnny Rivers, Johnny Mills, and Mr. Culpepper. I took Mrs. Anderson to my favorite spot, a world-renowned hole-in-the-wall that I thought harkened back to the three barbecue kings of the '30s. We dug into shoulder sandwiches. I held my breath and waited for her review. After an extended period of chewing, she matter-of-factly remarked, "They have a low overhead."

I finally built up the courage to ask about her first name. That label on her barbecue sauce and her formality about proper titles had made me wonder. She told me she changed the spelling from Annie to Annye as a teenager, and she now prefers the African pronunciation, On-yay. That was that. I still can't say it, and when I call her on the phone, I always identify myself as Mr. Lauterbach. I don't mind it. I find that I'm pretty susceptible to old-fashioned ways. I'd wear a wide-brimmed hat everywhere, no problem. She got into my head to the extent that I called other people Mr. or Mrs., but found it doesn't sit right with anyone else.

After meeting in Memphis, we got together every few months to work on the book, once for an interview Mrs. Anderson gave to two of Robert Johnson's distinguished biographers, Elijah Wald and Peter Guralnick. Their Q&A is included in this book, and as you'll see, humorous anecdotes and a musical breakthrough ensued.

I have to mention the person who helped bring me to this project—Mrs. Anderson's eldest daughter, Hughia. Mrs. Anderson wanted to hire a writer who knows 1930s Memphis, where she grew up with Robert Johnson. Hughia found out about my books and helped to connect me with her mother. I never had the chance to meet Hughia, though, as she passed away in February 2019. Hughia had said that Mrs. Anderson is every bit as important as Robert Johnson. I agree. Much more than her treasure or her association with Robert Johnson, I cherish Mrs. Anderson's voice. It's been my top priority to share her lovely figures of speech, witty turns of phrase, and warm, charming diction, along with biting commentary on race in America. Though I omitted her frequent use of the word "honey" as punctuation, I think the sweetness remains. It's not every day that you have the pleasure of listening to a person who's spent nearly a century keenly observing this world, a person whose father was born the year after slavery ended, and can tell us how far we haven't come.

And, her Robert Johnson stories aren't too shabby either. This book contains revelations surprising and delightful, insights about this legendary figure and his music that I don't think we fans expected to ever receive. Mrs. Anderson also tells the heartbreaking tale of how her family has been deprived of the rights to his music, even while white people who never knew him made money off of Robert Johnson. For Mrs. Anderson to share her story with us is a gift that I hope we deserve. With this act of courage and generosity, Mrs. Anderson restored my faith in the vitality of history. Almost every day, that faith is shaken when I read about first-evers or last-livings who have gone on. But just as soon as you think that the beautiful past really is dead, someone gently taps you on the forearm and says, "Honey, I'm on your time."

Brother Robert's People

Children of Charles Dodds Spencer (Robert's stepfather) and Julia Majors Dodds (Robert's mother)

Harriet Spencer Curry "Hattie"

Lula Spencer

Bessie Hines "Sister Bessie" (spouse of "Brother Granville" Hines)

Caroline Harris Thompson "Sister Carrie"

Charley Leroy Melvin Spencer "Son"

Children of Charles Dodds Spencer and Willie Spencer

James Spencer "Brother James"

Theodore Spencer

Children of Charles Dodds Spencer and Mollie Winston Spencer

Charlyne Spencer "Sister Charlyne"

Annye Clara Spencer Anderson

Siblings of Charles Dodds Spencer

Ida Cross "Aunt Ida," and Rev. William Cross (husband)

William Dodds "Brother" (my Uncle Will, lived on South Side of Chicago and owned a barbershop on the South Side)

Aaron Dodds (brother)

John Dodds (brother)

I

Growing Up with Robert Johnson

CHAPTER 1

I called him Brother Robert. He called me Baby Sis or Little Girl.

We weren't blood. We were family.

First time I remember Brother Robert, he helped us move to Memphis from the country in 1929. My little legs couldn't make it up the big staircase leading to our new house. I felt someone scoop me up and carry me. On his long, lanky legs, he took those steps two at a time. From then on, he was around sometimes for the rest of his life.

Those were the years Brother Robert was into his music. He used to sit out on those tall steps and pick his guitar, way up in the air. I saw him go from wearing patches to pinstripes, clodhoppers to Florsheims. I knew him when he supposedly agreed to his deal with the devil, while he made his records, right up to when the telegram came to our sister's house with the news that he had died.

I don't recognize the person in the stories other people tell. I can't say all he did or didn't do, I didn't have him in my pocket. But nobody else living today grew up with him as I did. I want people to know what the real Robert Johnson was like, how I remember him from my childhood. Some say he was a vagabond. They make it seem like he was alone in the world. He did hobo, but he was not without a loving family.

People don't understand that my family lost Brother Robert twice. Once when he was killed down in Mississippi. And again when money grabbers spread all these myths—stole our photographs and our memories and made money off of them. But our family survived many attacks over the years, and we've always been strong.

One attack on my family was the reason both me and Brother Robert came to be. Because really, neither one of us ever should have been born. It all began with a knife fight in Mississippi. This happened in 1906.

My father was one of the men in that fight. Charlie Dodds was his name. He became known as Charlie Spencer after what happened in Hazlehurst. He was born in 1866, the year after slavery ended.

My father always worked for himself. He ran a barbershop, did carpentry, construction, and built and upholstered furniture. He also cut and delivered firewood. I knew from an early age that my father's name was Dodds, not Spencer, and I knew why it was changed. My father was very open. I heard it from his mouth.

He took some wood to a woman's house. This white

guy Marchetti accosted my father and wanted to know what he was doing there. Well, this woman was a mulatto. My father said, "I'm talking to my own."

Marchetti had to know this woman wasn't white. In a town like that, everybody knows who's who. Marchetti may have been sweet on her. But my father was just delivering firewood. On that same evening, Marchetti came to my father's barbershop, accosted him, and cut him with a long blade knife on the left side of his jaw. Being a barber, my father carried a razor on his left side, and cut Marchetti back. You know my father wasn't getting away with that, although Marchetti was in the wrong.

My father knew the white man would be coming to do him further harm. He hurried home. He prepared a place to hide. He cut a tunnel into the thicket of a blackberry patch behind the house. If you could see those brambles, you'd know nobody could get in there. He crawled through those briars. My father said he could feel the ground shake with all the horses coming.

Sister Carrie, his youngest daughter, was three. She remembered the men in the posse asking, "Where's your father, little girl?" Well, she wouldn't know that at such a young age.

They would have lynched him. They didn't know he was right under their nose.

My father was married to Robert's mother at the time. I call her Mama Julia. I got to know her real well. She and my father married in February 1889.

I am told that right after the men left, Mama Julia prepared food and took it out to him. She knew that the next day would not be a good day.

The men continually stopped by the house looking for my father over the next several days. After almost two weeks, they gave up. Mama Julia was able to make contact with neighbors to help get my father out of Hazlehurst.

An escape route had to be planned and my father had to be camouflaged for his getaway. They had the idea to dress my father as a woman and sneak him on board a train. Mama Julia was very short, about 4'10"—her clothes couldn't conceal my father. A friend who was taller provided a dress, cloak, suitcase, and makeup suitable for a woman my father's size, about 5'5". He wore a size 10 shoe, so it took some time to find a woman's shoe to fit him.

Finally, with the help of loyal friends, my father purchased a train ticket. A family friend worked as a Pullman porter, and I wonder if he helped. My father went to the Hazlehurst station in disguise. He passed right by his would-be captors and entered the area of the train provided for Negroes. He'd brought his lunch, since the trains had no dining for black passengers. Not many Negroes rode at the time my father did, so he easily avoided having too many conversations. He made it safely to Memphis.

They had run him off his land. He had eight acres. I know that was disturbing. He left Mama Julia behind. He lost his home, lost his family, and I know that stayed with him, it was an aching thing. But he fought back. To this day, I'm glad my father stood up. My father was a man.

He healed very well. There were no keloids, but you could tell there was a cut.

A few years after the fight, Robert was born in the house my father built. By then my father had *been* gone.

He'd settled in Memphis, where he married his second wife, Willie, and had two children by her, James and Theodore Spencer. Willie died. I was told that Theodore, at age fifteen, had been beaten to death by a Memphis patrolman for allegedly stealing a bicycle. My brother James lived with my father until he was grown. I grew up with James around, until he left for Peoria, Illinois, and we never saw him again, but had contact for a while through the mail.

My father's third wife was my mother, Mollie Winston. They had two children together, my sister Charlyne, on December 27, 1923, and me, on April 20, 1926. My sister was named for my father. My mother named me after the nurse who cared for her at my birth.

Neither me nor Brother Robert would've come into this world without that knife fight at Hazlehurst. My father would have stayed with Mama Julia. He would never have met my mother, and Mama Julia never would have taken up with Robert's father. One documentary about Brother Robert states that my father abandoned Mama Julia. That wasn't the case. He had to run for his life.

We'd moved to Eudora, Mississippi, when I was a year old. My parents decided that they would sharecrop to support the family. My father had gotten up in age and found it difficult to earn money the way he once had. After a few years, my father had another altercation, this time with the landowner.

They had the boll weevil and the crops failed. The owner blamed my dad. He told my father, "If you weren't an old man, I'd kick you in your ass." Now, as a child, just over three years old at the time, this has to come from the memory of my parents talking, so a lot of my stories are handed down.

My father was a mild-mannered man, but he didn't take a lot of stuff. My father knew that his best bet was to move off of the property. And every sharecropper, if you read history, they had to move *at night*. Just leave. Mama Julia and Sister Carrie have had to do the same.

The landowner expected this. They'd come up front, look and see if you'd moved anything out. The furniture never moved up front, he always saw the same thing. There were certain furnishings moved to the back and taken out. Sister Carrie, she still lived in Memphis, and she made arrangements to move us. She had a friend named Charlie Gatewood, I'll never forget him. He had a truck. It took us several moves to get out, because the landlord always came by, checking and looking. Last thing before we left were the two mules my brother Son slapped and sent on back up the hill to the owner's home.

Son joked about this episode many times in later years. The mules were named Jake and Bell. We had our own cow, named Minnie, that we left behind with a black family named the Richmonds, who lived down the hill.

Brother Robert was there through it all. When he was young, Mama Julia would patch his overalls with anything she had. It'd be floral, striped, or whatever, may have been a piece of wool. She'd say, "It makes cleanness come." That's how he looked when I first remember seeing him.

He came from Sister Bessie's house in Robinsonville. Sister Bessie was the oldest living daughter of my father and Mama Julia. Brother Robert had to handle Patsy, our horse. Full-blooded Arabian. In those days the minister had what you call a saddle horse. Sister Bessie's husband, Brother Granville, was that kind of minister. He wore his black suit and derby hat and rode Patsy from house to house. He owned that horse, but got so he couldn't take care of it and he gave Patsy to my father. That horse knew Brother Robert very well, because he had been taking care of her at Sister Bessie's. Brother Robert came along to mind Patsy. Brother Robert stayed with that horse in Memphis until we arrived from Eudora.

This house we moved to in Memphis had four garages in the back. My father came up and prepared the second garage from the end for Patsy. My father carved a square out so Patsy could hang her head out the window. Brother Robert came up to take care of the horse, feed the horse.

We moved to 291 E. Georgia Avenue, a two-story yellow house. That's where Brother Robert carried me up the

Georgia Avenue from Hernando Street. Taken in 1940, this shows the neighborhood as Robert Johnson saw it. Second from right is the "big yellow house" where Johnson carried his "Baby Sis" up the stairs. At right is the field where ministers sermonized about the crossroads. *Photo courtesy of the Memphis Room, Memphis Public Library*

steps the first time. It was Sister Carrie's house. It was, to me, a very big house. Sister Carrie's son Lewis was there, and we played hide-and-seek. Sister Carrie had a little poodle that I was scared to death of, named Snowball.

I hope people can get to know the loved ones who were around Brother Robert in Memphis. That begins with Sister Carrie. A very sweet sister, she always helped the family out.

Sister Carrie was born in Hazlehurst, Mississippi, in 1903. Daddy and Mama Julia originally named her Caroline, but she didn't like the name and changed it to Carrie. She came to Memphis to live with our father a few years after the knife fight. Sister Carrie was the backbone of the family. Everybody went to her. She wasn't educated, but she was savvy about worldly things. She had to come out of school early, and she married at sixteen. She always wanted to finish school, but never had the chance.

Sister Carrie worked for herself as a seamstress and spent most of her life sewing. She's the best seamstress I've ever seen. She tailored. She made slipcovers. Sister Carrie could've been a top designer with opportunity. When my sister picked up a hem in a silk dress, you could hardly see it from the other side. In the Great Depression, people were not always buying a new suit, though. Sister Carrie would let their hems out, or redo them, turn the cuffs and collars where things got torn, she did a lot of that. Sister Carrie sewed for a Greek man we called Mr. Pete. He was part owner of the One Minute Café on Beale Street. He sold hotdogs. Sometimes I could get a free one. Brother Robert and Brother Son knew Mr. Pete very well. He'd bring us olives and olive oil.

Sister Carrie was fly—smart dresser, pretty woman. She was a chain smoker until the end, Camels and Chesterfields. Sometimes Bull Durham roll 'ems when she couldn't afford the higher brands. She helped to rear Brother Robert, and she bought him his first guitar. Sister

Carrie and my mother got along quite well, otherwise we wouldn't have been living together.

My mother, Mollie Spencer, was a hardworking woman, a Christian woman. She was born in Jackson, Mississippi, in 1898.

What you call snapping your fingers, my mother called finger poppin'. My mother didn't have any blues and finger poppin' in *her* house. I laugh today when I think of what my mother said about finger poppin' and dancing—"Heathens!"

She sang sweet songs like "This Little Light of Mine," "I'll Fly Away," and "I Wonder if the Lighthouse Will Shine on Me," and she would always talk about what a little birdie told her. I think Brother Robert got that idea of having a bird to whistle and a bird to sing in "Stones in My Passway" from my mother.

I've never known her to go to church. She said, "I don't have the clothes, and people will look down on you if you're not in the right hat." I've only seen my mother dress when I got in trouble at school. She had to come talk to the teacher. She'd won eighteen dollars at policy, that's what we called the numbers game. A black man would come through collecting bets. Sinners and saints played policy. In the Great Depression, we all had to make that money. We saw the same man every day, a tall dark-skinned black man. Evidently, the policy collectors had their routes. My mother played the same number. She only won once, and bought a nice black coat. I gave the coat to a close neighbor after my mother died.

My mother didn't like blues at all, she thought it low class. All around her, we liked the blues. She told us, "No gamblin' and no midnight ramblin'."

She brought us up right. We used to think she was the meanest woman in the world. Sister Carrie said, "One day you'll appreciate this." We'd complain to Sis Carrie because she was fly and younger. If my mother got too hard on us, my father said, "That'll do, Mollie." He did not whip us and did not believe in whipping children.

She did have a sense of humor. My mother said when the gypsies come by to tell our fortune, never let them in. She said to tell them that if she didn't work for what she got, she already knew her fortune—that she wouldn't have shit. My mother allowed us to say that to the gypsies. They never came back.

My mother was very kind. We fed the hobos, even if all we had was an old cold biscuit. We've had black folks to drop in on the house and say, "I'm hungry." We set them at the table and fed them. Whether they were telling the truth or not, they were fed anyway. I remember at one time, my mother fed a family of four. And with a gilded heart, she sent them home with a basket of food.

Brother Robert loved my mother's food, her barbecue sauce, her chowchow and vegetables. My mother was uneducated but she knew about pH. She made some chowchow, it was smackin' good. Little Richard didn't coin the phrase "Good Golly Miss Mollie," because that's what Brother Robert would say when he ate my mother's chowchow. When Brother Robert came around, he didn't starve, and he loved to eat and could really put it away. He called my mother "Miss Mollie," even when he didn't say "Good golly."

My mother's sister, Aunt Mary, lived around us in Memphis, too. Aunt Mary did her thing. She and Sister Carrie went out to the juke joints. They were running buddies. But I can remember Aunt Mary loving her spirituals. She sang, "Soon, so soon, I'm going to see the King, Lord I wouldn't mind dying if dying was all." She died young in surgery at John Gaston Hospital in Memphis. She gave me lots of hugs and kisses. She was a Bingham, married to my uncle Albert. She did domestic work and lived in an apartment in our neighborhood.

A lot of people don't know, but Brother Robert learned to play guitar at the knee of my father. Seven years old, when he came to my father.

My father played many instruments: guitar, fiddle, banjo, mandolin. He wasn't against finger-poppin' at all, 'cause he did it himself, played the devil's music. He had earned his living, partially, playing music at frolics in Mississippi during his younger years. On Fridays and Saturdays that's what he did: "I Was Seeing Nellie Home," "Turkey in the Straw." Nobody knows that my father was a musician. He loved so-called worldly music. His main instrument was the fiddle. He loved to listen to Fiddlin' John Carson and Uncle Dave Macon on the radio.

When he was teaching Brother Robert, I hadn't been born. I got that from Sister Carrie. Evidently my father quit music when he married my mother 'cause she wasn't having that barrelhouse stuff in her house. But after my father parted from Mama Julia and before he married my mother, he kept Brother Robert. I believe that I have heard Brother Robert call my father "Papa."

One day in 1918, Sister Carrie went to Front Street in Memphis. She happened to see Mama Julia and said, "That looks like my mother." Brother Robert was with Mama Julia. I know Mama Julia must have been looking for my father. That's when times were hard. I imagine Sister Carrie was happy to see her mother, happy to meet Brother Robert. And that's how Brother Robert got to my father's house. Mama Julia left him there. My father and Mama Julia's oldest living daughters, Hattie and Lula, had come to Memphis, and they were around Brother Robert, too. Mama Julia couldn't feed herself and take care of her child. He needed overseeing and she couldn't do it. She went from plantation to plantation making her living cropping and picking cotton.

My father taught Robert Johnson the rudiments of music. My father reared Brother Robert while living on Court Avenue at Dunlap Street in Memphis. My mother was a laundress working in that area when she met my father. He made very good money at that time as a self-employed carpenter, builder, and roofer.

After a while, Sister Carrie was the only one taking care of Brother Robert. My father and Mama Julia's daughters Sister Hattie and Sister Lula had died. Sister Carrie had her son Lewis the same year Sister Hattie died, in 1920. Brother Robert was becoming—you may have heard the term—mannish. He may have become hard to handle, or wanted to start doing things Sister Carrie couldn't oversee. In his teens, Brother Robert learned that my father wasn't his real father. This is how I interpret them sending him back to his mother. My father sent him there. He was never without his mother, even when he lived with my father, and Mama Julia came and lived with Sister Carrie for a time.

People said, "Your father's old," but honey, he was a father. He was a smart man and my mother always said he didn't have a lazy bone in his body. There's nothing he couldn't do. We never suffered. We never had a food shortage. We fed the neighbors, even though they stole from his garden.

My father worked right on up until two weeks before he died. I wish he and my mother could have lived to see what I've become and what I could've done for them. That's the only thing that I wish. I still have my father's hammer with his initials carved on it, C.D.

My father and Mama Julia's oldest boy, Charles Leroy Spencer, was born in Hazlehurst in 1895. Everybody called him "Son." In the house in Hazlehurst, my father had an organ and a piano. He taught Son guitar. Son was a pianist, too. Son played well—jazz, country, and blues. He loved his country music. I come from a black family that loved country music.

Louis Armstrong, Fats Waller, Jimmie Lunceford, and Duke Ellington were household words. That's my brother

Son's thing. Son mimicked Louis Armstrong with that growling voice and clowned like Fats Waller. Son would tell me my feets too big, that's what Fats Waller used to sing. He played "Honeysuckle Rose," "Darktown Strutters Ball," and "I'm Gonna Sit Right Down and Write Myself a Letter."

Brother Son was very close to Brother Robert, so Brother Robert got some of his nicks and picks from Son, because my father wasn't as current as Son became. Son sang "Poor Boy a Long Way from Home," "Highway 61," as some of his favorites, and "44 Blues." Son played "The Dirty Dozens" and "When the Evening Sun Go Down," and "Blues Before Sunrise." Being older, Son liked ragtime, and knew how to play "Maple Leaf Rag," and "Alexander's Ragtime Band."

Son lived off and on with Sister Carrie. Son was very talented and smart, he just didn't do anything with himself. He worked for Kraft in Memphis during the Great Depression. Whatever Kraft sold, mayonnaise and relish, we got it, because he could bring some of the products home. Brother Robert called him "Son" and also called him by his middle name, "Leroy." Son liked dark-skinned women, he used that saying "the blacker the berry, the sweeter the juice."

Aunt Ida was my father's baby sister. She was married to Rev. William Cross, a minister. At least he thought he was a minister. He didn't have his own church. Back then we called them jacklegs. Sister Carrie and Mr. Cross had a business together, and he stole her blind, the old skunk. Aunt Ida and Rev. Cross lived in the neighborhood. They visited us often, and dined with us during the Thanksgiving and Christmas holidays.

My older sister Charlyne, my only full sibling, and my father's son Brother James, by his second marriage, were around, too. My Brother James was a junkman, that's how he made his living. Patsy became a workhorse during the Great Depression after we moved up from Eudora—James used Patsy to drive his wagon. Brother Robert was close to Brother James. They used to ride to Beale Street with Patsy pulling the wagon, hats turned backwards, which was the style among young black men at that time.

Sister Carrie's son Lewis, born in 1920, also became very close to Brother Robert. Lewis is gone, but his son is still alive. He might be the last definite blood relative of Robert Johnson that the family has known. Robert's mother would have been great-grandmother to Lewis's boy. Lewis's first son died shortly after birth. We called him "Butternut" because he was plump.

Lewis did not finish high school. He lied about his age to join the navy. But he attended the same schools I attended, Kortrecht Grammar and Booker T. Washington High. Lewis always made good grades. I still have some of his report cards. He could read music, and I used to have his sheet music that he wrote.

So it comes back to me. I am not a first-name person. I grew up in a time when white people were always addressed as "Mister," "Missus," or "Mizz," and blacks were called boy, girl, uncle, auntie, or worse. People, even black people, don't always know why I refer to "Sister" Carrie and "Brother" Robert—they were much older than me. To me, a first name is awfully fresh. Being on a first-name basis is designed to avoid giving black people the respect they're due. Using a first name is a privilege and not a right. But back then everyone called me "Annie Clara."

When I was nine years old, my mother had to live on a place and chop and pick cotton to make ends meet, and I stayed with a schoolteacher named Miss Blanche Billings in Hollywood, North Memphis. My mother picked cotton, and if she didn't pick three hundred pounds, it wasn't a good day. Miss Billings taught me my first table manners. She would set a formal table and teach me how to hold a fork and how to set the table. She taught me how to address a person, "Yes, Miss Billings." None of that sassy "yes," or "yes ma'am." Most people don't get it. I later had difficulty with my husband's parents, because they kept our children and taught them to say "yes'm" and "no'm" but I wouldn't have it—you address the person by name.

My memories get stronger around the time my family left the big yellow house and moved to the backhouse next door, 285, rear, E. Georgia Avenue. I grew up in that house. We stayed there from 1932, for the rest of Brother Robert's life, until my father died in 1940. The house still stands today, vacant and dilapidated. It ought to be a historical site. I stood in the doorway, and, though it looked broken inside, I could still see where my mother canned her beans, where my father smoked his pipe, and I gazed at the steps where Brother Robert used to play next door where Sister Carrie once lived.

The whole neighborhood that I recall being so lively is like the house, broken up and only alive in memory.

CHAPTER 2

Children were devilish, and I was among them, no angel—
but the old folks thought I was. I got into some fights.
Sister Carrie and my mother taught me to hit, but only to
hit back and never to throw the first lick. I was a skinny
child, but well built and strong. Everybody talked about
the athletic figure that I had. I danced and I skipped, and
I jumped rope. So I was in good shape. And we walked
everywhere, didn't have bus fare. I did that for years and I
was never flabby. I wore Buster Brown shoes and pleated
dresses.

I'd be up *early* in the morning, trying to find someone to play with, or some little work to do. My big sister
Charlyne stayed in the house, reading. I got into everything around the neighborhood and met everyone. When
we'd first come up from Eudora, I heard a baby crying in
one of the houses and went up to see that baby. It turned

out to be the house where the Comas family lived, and they knew my father from Hazlehurst.

There was Brother Pete, whose real name was Robert Comas, who was my father's age, and his wife, Willie. Brother Pete and my father grew up near each other and had gone to school together. Brother Pete and Willie's son, Mr. Martzie Comas, was very tall, and his wife, Marie, was short. They loved blues, we had a good time with them. Mr. Martzie was older than Brother Robert, but they were friends. Martzie and Marie had a son, little Bobby, he was the baby in the crib when I first moved in from Eudora. Then they had Billy, next was Betty, I was close to all of them. Then Eugene, we called him "Tunka." Son would dress up Tunka, slick his hair back, and carry Tunka around in his arms. Then was "Tinka." They couldn't say "Annie Clara," they called me "Annie Slara." The Comas family eventually left Memphis for California, and there's some out there still.

They were like our family. The Comases lived on Georgia Avenue and, later, on the next street around the corner from us, on Hernando. Brother Robert played many a house party at the Comas place. They had a piano that Brother Pete's wife Willie would play. Son played that piano, too. Everyone who liked blues would come to those house parties.

Georgia Avenue was quiet, mostly family oriented. Everyone had a house, a yard. Some big homes had been converted into apartments, and everyone took on boarders. Music played everywhere. You had a few people who were different that lived in what my mother called bad houses. We knew where the bad houses were. And you didn't associate. A few doors down, you could hear them playing "Big Leg Woman" by Johnny Temple on a Sunday. There's culture within the culture among black people. We don't all go in for the same things. Mr. Martzie's aunt had a bad house, with everything. His wife would accuse him of meeting another woman over there. I remember a fight Mr. Martzie and Mrs. Marie had, when she called the policeman, but she ended up jumping on the policeman.

Lola Myers was the blues lady in the neighborhood, at 275 E. Georgia Avenue. She played records, "It's Tight Like That," by Tampa Red, I remember. My mother heard me singing that song, and said, "Don't sing that song." Ms. Myers's place wasn't a bad house, she just needed to play her blues at times, for therapy.

There was a field on the other side of her house, which went west all the way to Georgia and Third Street—also known as Highway 61. Mrs. Haley lived at 249 E. Georgia and had a daughter who sang religious songs, sometimes on the radio. A Baptist preacher named Rev. Edward Payne used to go visit the Haleys and Lola Myers all the time in his Terraplane. I think it was dark green. Most people didn't have cars, so that Terraplane stood out, parked on Georgia Avenue.

East on Georgia, whites lived on a hill. It was just an elevated place. All that's left of their big houses are the bricks of yesteryear. We had Jewish, Irish, and Italian. But

Mrs. Annye C. Anderson outside of her family home. Memphis, 2018.
Photo by Preston Lauterbach

everybody was poor and it was a saying, "they're still here because they couldn't afford to move out."

None of them socialized with black people, but we were out picking the wild greens together in the field in back of our house. We picked calaloo, peppergrass—similar to creasy greens—lamb's quarters, purslane, plantain. The greens came up as perennial—poke salad, it's in the spinach family. Now people are really getting into these wild plants. During the Great Depression, that's what we ate.

In Memphis, the white kids were given thirty minutes or maybe an hour to get out and get home from school before black children at school were let out. That was to protect them from *usses*. Memphis was very segregated. Reason I know, we were friends with the Kellys, an Irish family. They'd come by our house long before we even got out of school.

I only can go by hearsay on Brother Robert's education, but he had to go to school. I never heard where, and my family lived in a different neighborhood in Memphis back before I came along.

We worked together during the Depression. To tell you how close we were, when Mrs. Kelly had her last baby, her three boys came and slept on pallets in our kitchen while she was in labor. We grew hay for Mrs. Kelly's cow, Flossy. We got butter from her and they gave us what cream and milk they could afford. My mother canned chili beans, barbecue sauce, and pickles, and she'd send me with some to Mrs. Kelly's. She had two big dogs I was afraid of, a male and female, King and Queen. Me and her daughter Margaret got into all kinds of devilment.

Mr. Kelly worked on the railroad. Just what he did, I don't know, but he used to carry that rag in his back pocket. He used to tell Brother Robert, "You ride the train more than I do."

They lived on Carolina Avenue, one street south, parallel to Georgia on the other side of a field where my father gardened above our house. He planted peas, beans, corn, and sorghum up on the hill, and all the way to the train track from the bayou. When the hobos got off the train, they had to walk through my father's field. It started at the dead end of Carolina, all the way to the bayou, which was in front of our house. He had a beautiful garden. My father kept it weedless. Everywhere you stepped, you'd see a footprint.

My father grew and enclosed collard greens and cabbage year round, because the weather lent itself to that. He'd use a tarpaulin and put it on stakes, and cover the vegetables, because we had some heavy snow at times. In the front of the yard we grew lettuce and we always had our premium herbs.

My father was really into his herbs. He treated a neighbor woman for diabetes with mullein. We used sweet elm for a toothbrush, soda for toothpaste and underarm deodorant. You chew the sweet elm and it makes into a brush. That's all we had. I never will forget, my father would treat a burn with honey and soda, and it'd heal very nicely. He made sassafras tea for other ailments.

Past the Caucasians' hill, you come to Fourth Street. At Georgia and Fourth you got groceries at Lazarov's. Next door, Pete's Place served hotdogs and hamburgers. It was a short-order restaurant. That's where we played records. He had blues, Sonny Boy Williamson, later, after Brother Robert was gone, we played Tommy McClennan. "Bottle Up and Go."

Every Saturday I got a quarter for picking up a chicken for a lady living at Georgia and Fourth. She had a daughter who was challenged and, so, needed me to shop for her. She wanted fresh chicken but was scared to kill it. Russo's, up towards Fifth Street, had the fresh chicken. I'd carry it to her in a bag. And I'd also wring the neck. I'd seen my father do that. That was a set quarter, that was my show fare. A show cost a nickel, and then the price went up to a dime. That was a little high, because I used to pay my neighbors Puddin' and Beatcha's fare.

As children, we could only go as far as Fifth, to some houses that looked like mansions but were turned into apartments. Son and Brother Robert played there. We

Railroad bridge where Robert Johnson caught the train, Hernando Street. Memphis, 2018. *Photo by Preston Lauterbach*

could go to Russo's just over Fifth. My mother always said, "Whenever that streetlight comes on, you come home."

Our pathway came alongside of the house past the cellar and was lined with Mexican burning bushes all the way down to the bayou. Those hedges separated us from the path that Brother Robert and the hobos would use, coming down from the train. They'd jump off at Hernando and Carolina. There's a switch at Hernando Street, and Brother Robert told me never to play around there because he knew a man who got his legs cut off there at the switch.

My father built a hogpen and a small smokehouse near Patsy's stall in our yard. Our house sat right on the bayou. It was a small duplex with two front doors and two front steps.

My father had his old barber chair in a corner of the front room. He sat there every evening when he came in, back of his potbelly stove. Above the stove my father had hung pictures of his brothers, my Uncle John and Uncle Aaron, in gilded frames. My father couldn't pass for white, but they could, and I often wondered why we had those white folks up there. He had *The Last Supper* hanging on one wall, and Michelangelo's hands from the Sistine Chapel on another. He'd smoke his pipe, and once in a while he'd reach up and get his Old Grand-Dad. Not every day, because I didn't have any drinking parents. He took his nip on rock candy—he dipped crystal candy in his whiskey. My mother liked her wine, but only served it with cake on the holidays. My mother made her wine and

Inside the Spencer home, where Robert Johnson stayed with family. Memphis, 2018. *Photo by Preston Lauterbach*

brandy—dandelion, blackberry, grape, and peach brandy. We'd get plenty of dandelion flowers way off the road.

We didn't have a radio in our house, we didn't have electricity. Our water at 285 E. Georgia was outside, the toilet was outside. We had good drinking water, artesian water.

We had a white hobo named Crip living in our shed for a number of years. Our neighbors wanted to know why we didn't put him out, but I guess my father remembered when he was on the run. He was a fugitive at one time. Crip never bothered anybody, but he was an alcoholic. We gave him old army blankets, and he'd sleep out on the hay. He did that for a number of years. My father went out one day, found him dead, and had to call the policeman. My father often said, "You are your brother's keeper."

When Sister Carrie got so she couldn't pay the rent on that big house at 291 Georgia, she moved right next to us. My parents lived on one side of the duplex and Sister Carrie lived on the other. I learned that Sister Carrie slept with a pistol under her pillow, and I know it was a .32. I think that's what Brother Robert sang about, his sister's .32. I know she could shoot. She was soft-spoken and tiny, but to live alone, she knew how to protect herself.

We stayed close with our family in Mississippi. Brother Robert's mother, Mama Julia, and my mother had had the same husband, but they were friends. I can hear Mama Julia now. "I have nothing against Mollie, because she never did anything to me." She knew my mother met my father long after he had to leave. Mama Julia married a man called Mr. Willis, a farmer down in Mississippi. He was religious, anti-blues, like Mama Julia and my mother. So Mr. Willis, my father, my mother, and Mama Julia, I've seen them sitting out in the yard talking. I don't know what they talked about, but they visited us often. People thought it strange, but we had to feed one another during the Great Depression, and we had a good relationship.

My father sent the sorghum he grew down to Robins-ville, Mississippi, for our molasses to be made. He sent his corn to Mississippi for hominy grits and cornmeal to be made. Mama Julia and Sister Bessie ground it, and sent it back to us. Mama Julia and Sister Bessie gave us, each September, a shoat. We fattened it up until late February or early March, and they came up to help us kill it. We cured ham, made hogshead souse, and pickled the pig's feet. Brother Robert's favorite foods included chitterlings and hog maws. We called fried chitterlings "ruffled delights." Brother Robert wasn't a country boy, but he'd come with them at hog-killing time, his mother, Mister Willis, Sister Bessie, and Brother Granville.

I lived with Brother Granville after Sister Bessie came to Memphis to have surgery. My mother let us go down. We were young, I was in grammar school. Sister Bessie's house was elevated because of floodwaters. The house had a little porch above the steps. It was an old wooden house, off the dirt road. That road had the most beautiful clay dust, where the river had overflowed and washed that silt in front of the house.

Family friends Mr. Clark and Mrs. Belton lived across the way, sort of diagonally. Mrs. Belton was a dear and close friend of my mother's and the entire family. Mrs. Belton lived directly across from Sister Bessie's house. Where they lived was nothing but cottonfields and dust. My mother visited Mrs. Belton often. Mrs. Belton had a cow. That woman thought I didn't get enough to eat, so she'd go out and milk that cow while I was there and bring the milk in for me to drink. It'd be that warm milk. I thought I'd go crazy. But she was a fine woman, and very close to Mama Julia and all the rest of the family. Mama Julia lived in the same territory, but a good distance away from Sister Bessie's house.

Mama Julia lived off a back road that went a good distance to her house. I would go down and visit Mama Julia, when they had the rally at her church. You talk about a one-egg cake, if they couldn't put together three eggs to make a pound cake, they'd use one. The church was near her house and they used to have rallies, where Brother Granville would preach. She belonged to Knights of Tabor. She always tied her little stuff up in a handkerchief, including her bible, which I still have in my possession.

Brother Granville used to holler out in the field, when he was behind the plow. It sounded like what Brother Robert's doing in "Terraplane." I can still hear Brother Granville singing "Guide Me O, Thou Great Jehovah." You heard that humming like Brother Robert does in "Come on in My Kitchen" in those old Baptist hymns.

Mama Julia could sing. She was a little woman, about four-foot-ten, but had a powerful voice. She didn't even need a microphone in church. She had more energy than any little woman I've ever seen. Even at age eighty, when she died. She was busy, busy, busy, she never stopped. Whatever you're doing she wanted to help. Quilting was her thing. If you see her hands, they're long and nimble like Brother Robert's. Brother Robert had that old church feeling in his singing. His mother could belt out.

Despite what happened to his mother, and having to give him up, he loved his mother. And she loved her "boy."

She usually called him Bob, my boy, or Robert, she would address him by those three. She would often say she made a mistake, but the Lord forgave her a long time ago. Mama Julia had him out of wedlock, but she was a devout Christian. She had great faith and was sincere. I never heard Mama Julia say who Robert's father was. Sister Carrie said she would see her mother sitting in the swing with a man. She didn't know him either.

During this time, Brother Robert began to branch out, lived on and off with Sister Carrie, with his mother, or Sister Bessie. He's been called lazy because he aspired to do something more than pick and chop cotton and say yes-suh and nosuh to white folks.

He didn't like farm work, so he had to come to the city. But he was restless and didn't stay long. Sweet as he was, I've come to think that maybe bitterness drove him. You have to understand that about Brother Robert.

When Brother Robert came to town, he was king. Sister Carrie ordered his first guitar from Sears & Roebuck and paid for it. It's my understanding from her mouth. He didn't have any money, so he had to get it from somebody.

He never stayed in my mother's side of the house. On Sister Carrie's side, he could pick his guitar. You could pop your fingers all you want in her house. But my mother wouldn't have had it on her steps or in the house. On the bayou there was a platform that extended out onto the water. In front of our house, he would sit there and play his guitar. If they haven't torn it down, it's still there.

The front step at Sister Carrie's apartment, where Robert Johnson sat and played guitar. Memphis, 2019. *Photo by Preston Lauterbach*

For a while he wore his patched overalls. Then he had the khakis, starched and creased. Son would do that for him. Son could press. I've never seen Brother Robert iron, everything was done for him. He played the guitar—he was the star of the show. I've never seen him cook, everything was cooked for him.

Brother Robert loved to eat and never gained a pound. He loved fried pumpkin. Making ends meet, that's a delicious dish. You use butter, if you could afford it, and we always had bacon grease, to mix in with the butter. You boil the pumpkin first. Your spices are on the sweet side. You mix all your spices together and the sugar, and you add it until the pumpkin thickens. We called that roping. You can drop it in the mixture until the pumpkin dries out. It was just delicious. That could be a dessert. He stayed slender, kept that boyish figure though he'd eat and eat and eat. My mother would feed him, but there wouldn't be any blues in her house.

In 1934, my mother took a job at a café nearby, Friendly Lunch Room, over on Hernando Street at Calhoun Avenue. That became an important place for my family— Brother Robert picked his guitar at that café.

The Smith family ran the place. They'd been around the neighborhood for as long as we'd lived there. They moved into the upstairs of the big yellow house at 291 E. Georgia after we left. Alice Smith and my mother were best friends. The Smiths' daughter Geneva was one of my best friends. Of course the Smiths knew all about my mother's cooking.

The Smith café, strictly a soul food restaurant, served black-eyed peas, candied yams, collard greens, spaghetti, pigtails, oxtails, ham hocks and skins, fried chicken, smothered pork chops, fried catfish, chitterlings, and buffalo fish. My mother made barbecue pork shoulder and ribs, and she was second cook. My mother made the barbecue sauce, and my father grew the herbs, vegetables, and fruit that went into the barbecue sauce.

From the sidewalk on Hernando Street, steps led into the front door of the café. You had the counters along the walls and the Seeburg jukebox at the back. I remember Johnny Temple records playing, his music was ribald. Black blues was not played on the radio.

The building was elongated and pretty wide, shotgun style, with wood floors. There was a side door you could come in from Calhoun, about midway in the room. People smoked everywhere and there may have been a spittoon, because people spat everywhere. The place served beer. The kitchen was in the back. It had a huge backyard and they had a dog back there that bit me. I wasn't supposed to go back there, but Geneva and I were devils, she invited me back there and I was dumb enough to go. Well, the dog wasn't going to bite her, because it knew her.

That's the first public place I've seen Brother Robert play to an audience. It had benches all around the side of the restaurant on the north and west, and people would always come and sit. Brother Robert played "Little Boy Blue" and "Sittin' on Top of the World."

I stopped by the café with friends on our way home from school. People came from Beale Street, hangers-around, and sat on the benches. We were able to sit on stools at the counter and eat, but we had to leave after that.

Mrs. Smith had another daughter, seven years older than my sister and nine years older than me. We called her Miss B. She was a very pretty woman. Light-skinned, nice head of hair, if you know the term. Not too big, she never got fat. She dressed well. I couldn't hang around the café long, but I did notice Miss B and Brother Robert together there quite often.

If you turn over the original of his famous pinstripe suit photo, you'd see a note in Robert's handwriting: "To Miss B.M."

Miss B's real name was Bernice West. I don't know what the "M" stood for. We all knew her well and loved her. She went to Lemoyne, got her degree, and became a social worker. I know that by now—she's nine years older than me—she's gone on. Miss B is who Brother Robert sang about in "Walking Blues": *I feel like blowin' my ol' lonesome home, got up this morning my little Bernice was gone.*

I would run into Miss B several times over the years to come.

In that same song, Brother Robert sings about riding the blinds. That too comes from his life. Brother Robert rode the blinds. That didn't have to mean a cattle car, I'm talking about anywhere a person can't see. Could be on the running board, and if the wind is blowin', he'd ride backwards. My mother picked cotton and chopped cotton, and they'd pick you up at dark in the morning to take you to Arkansas or Mississippi. If Brother Robert was available, he'd take that ride to Hernando, or that ride across the bridge to Arkansas, and he wasn't going to pick cotton. He wouldn't get a seat inside, under the canopy. Riding the blinds is hitching a ride and catching on wherever you can't see.

I never knew where he was going when he left.

CHAPTER 3

I turned ten years old in April of 1936. After that my little world began to grow. My mother hadn't allowed me to hang around Beale Street. Prostitutes were everywhere during that time. Close by in some of the private homes, I have seen whites come out and pick up black women. I imagine everything happened on Beale Street. That's why my parents didn't want me down there. I was told never to go to Handy Park, they had everything over there, gambling, the bluesmen were over there. Brother Robert went over there when he got ready. That was a proving ground.

Little by little, I ventured farther from home and got to know the way to Beale. My old territory between Third and Fifth, Calhoun and the railroad, was only about two or three blocks each way. Beale Street was almost a mile from the house, but easy to reach, straight up Hernando Street.

My ticket out came from Sister Carrie, through Brother Robert. She got her buttons, thimbles, tape, and thread from Schwab's, a big general store on Beale. Sister Carrie stayed behind that sewing machine day and night and sometimes she needed supplies. She tried sending Brother Robert out, but he'd never come back. I had to go and find him. When I got to Beale, I knew he was playing his guitar, I could hear it coming up the street. I knew his riffs. Nobody else was playing like Brother Robert.

I have learned that he was contemporary while the others played classic blues. Wasn't any Duke Ellingtons out on the street. Everybody was exposed to blues. The jug bands paraded through our neighborhood, and the children would follow just like the pied piper. They marched with their jugs and all that. Children danced to the music. Brother Robert took no interest. He wanted modern. Brother Robert didn't sound like the jug bands or the Tampa Red I heard coming out of Ms. Lola Myers's house. He worked to distinguish himself.

When Brother Robert went to Beale Street, he ended up playing in Handy Park. He and Son teamed up and played there as a duo, as well. He was well known at the One Minute Café, next door to the Palace on Beale, and played there, thanks to my family's friendship with Mr. Pete, part-owner of the café.

A block east of Handy Park was Church's Park, named after Robert Church, the South's first black millionaire and real founder of Beale Street. While Handy Park could be a little rough, Church's Park appealed to the entire community. Teachers often held educational programs there and rehearsed and staged school plays in the auditorium.

Children could go and get some athletic instruction. One professor taught boys to box, including Sister Carrie's son Lewis, who became a professional welterweight. The park had a public pool for black kids, though no lifeguards. The atmosphere there would be upbeat and wholesome. Brother Robert met up with his buddies. They read the paper and learned about the politics of the day. Robert Church Jr. was one of the leading black politicians of the time, and he had a strong presence. Brother Robert would learn about the news from Ethiopia and hear about people like Paul Robeson, Marian Anderson, and Paul Laurence Dunbar. Of course everyone idolized Joe Louis and saw his victories as something bigger than boxing, and you could speak safely about such topics at Church's Park. Brother Robert had a girlfriend in that area named Pearl. She was dark brown with a gold crown on her front teeth, slender and about five-foot-six.

Once I got to go to Beale Street, I'd tag along with Brother Robert, Brother Son, and Sister Carrie to the movies at the Palace Theater. They liked to see Mae West and Bette Davis, and I was a nuisance, always running to the bathroom and wanting popcorn.

Most of the movies we saw at the Palace were Westerns. Buck Jones and Tom Mix were Brother Robert's favorite cowboys. He wore that big Stetson, like them. All of the young men in our family wore Stetson—that was on the go. My father and Uncle Will wore Dobbs.

At the Palace, Son and Brother Robert saw Gene Autry in *Tumbling Tumbleweeds*. Gene and another guitar player did a song called "That Silver-Haired Daddy of Mine."

That piece became a part of Son and Brother Robert's repertoire whenever they entertained.

All the top bands, Count Basie, Lionel Hampton, Lucky Millinder, Cab Calloway, and Jimmie Lunceford played at the Palace. We could see big entertainment for a small price. These acts also played the Orpheum, the grand opera theater on Main Street at Beale, one of the few integrated venues in the city, though blacks sat in the balcony.

It's my understanding that Brother Robert would hang out at the Palace while waiting on his next gig. Mr. Barrasso, the owner, let you stay all day on one ticket price. Brother Robert would sleep while the movie played over and over, and the *Looney Tunes*, shorts, and newsreels ran. He'd sit with the guitar across his chest, watching the old-time cowboy movies. He'd cool off in there on a hot day or warm up on a cold day until the time to meet up with his friends or return to Sister Carrie's.

Apart from going to Beale Street, another factor opened up my world—Sister Carrie had moved around the corner to 728 Hernando. That block came to a dead-end at the railroad, right where the tracks switched. We called that block Short Hernando. It had potholes, broken glass strewn about, some manicured yards, some not. Some people owned their homes, some did not. It wasn't far off, but it wasn't next door to my mother anymore either. My mother had two friends, Maybelle and Beulah, and when those three women got together, Lord have mercy, I could go to Halifax and come back. When I would go off and get into trouble, it'd still get back to my mother. I wondered how and she told me "I have a bird to whistle and a bird to sing." The old neighbors were like the Pony Express, they could deliver a message about me to my mother before I even got home from what I was doing.

728 Hernando is where Sister Carrie lived when Brother Robert's first recording was played, and where many house parties and yard parties were held. I felt free around my sister. I could pop and twist. Sis Carrie had an upstairs apartment, with the toilet on the porch between two other apartments. Wasn't any modern stuff. She did have a radio and a big wind-up Victrola record player. I would whine, I wanted to hear "Waiting for a Train." She'd have to get off her sewing machine and wind that Victrola. I'd whine and she'd mock me.

Since we could be free there, Carrie's became home to our music. Me and Brother Robert used to buckdance. Sister Carrie laughed at my spindly legs going everywhere. Son and Brother Robert liked listening to Clyde McCoy, a recording artist who had a regular gig at the Hotel Claridge in Memphis. Son and Brother Robert used to get close to the radio when he'd come on. He played "Sugar Blues," and I don't know how he'd wind that horn up, but they loved it. The radio was in the kitchen, and Sister Carrie would be in there sewing. They really would get down.

After Sister Carrie finished her work, and the sewing had been delivered, Sister Carrie would sing Bing Crosby songs and Brother Robert would strum "Did You Ever See a Dream Walking," and "Pennies from Heaven." She loved blues, and he played for her while she sang, "You've Been a Good Old Wagon" like Bessie Smith, and "Am I Blue?" like Ethel Waters.

On radio, we listened to WSM. We didn't miss Grand Ole Opry. I remember on a Saturday, my father saying, "Annie Clara, Robert is here." I was slow doing my chores, until I heard him say that. My father would take me to Sister Carrie's to see Brother Robert and listen to the Opry. I remember my father, an old fiddler, saying that Uncle Dave Macon was the best. My father and Brother Robert were very friendly with each other, crowding around and listening to the radio. My father was very much in favor of Brother Robert's music.

I know them all, Ernest Tubb. Fiddlin' John Carson, the Carter Family. Brother Robert and my favorite was Jimmie Rodgers. We had that record "Waiting for a Train." I sang that with Brother Robert all the time. Sister Carrie had the one by Charlie Patton about the crowing rooster, he said something about a rooster that crowed before day. And I would listen to that because it was about a chicken, but nothing could take the place of the trainman, Jimmie Rodgers.

I learned to sing along with those Jimmie Rodgers records. I couldn't yodel, but I'd sort of hum it. Brother Robert could really yodel. He identified with Jimmie Rodgers through the "TB Blues"—we had two older half-siblings die of TB in Memphis around the time Jimmie Rodgers passed from it.

In addition to yodeling, Brother Robert had other talents. He could play with both hands. He played his guitar back of his back. Brother Robert could play spoons, too. And when he was blowin' his harmonica, he played a tune I identify with DeFord Bailey on Grand Ole Opry. He could blow like a train chugging down the track. People don't know how deeply he was into country music. That was always a part of his repertoire.

Roy Acuff was popular with "The Great Speckled Bird." A Metropolitan Insurance agent used to come through the neighborhood, collecting payments. He'd stop in at Sister Carrie's. The insurance man played the guitar, and he and Son would sit down and pick. He was Caucasian and younger. I don't remember his name, but he and Son were really into Roy Acuff. The Metropolitan man sold burial insurance. Most black folks want to be put away nicely. We all had the burial, and could get it for a nickel or a dime per week. That was very important to us as black people.

Sister Carrie supported Brother Robert in so many ways. Brother Robert had a lot of white customers who brought him around. They called it slumming. He made connections through Sister Carrie. She sewed for upscale white hotels, the Claridge, Peabody, and Gayoso. Some people lived at the hotels. She'd let them know Brother Robert was in town. Son delivered the goods she sewed to the hotels, and snuck Brother Robert in with him. That's why we called Brother Robert the "backdoor man." These places were strictly segregated—a black person couldn't go and socialize among whites. Garfield Thompson, who we called Pops, another neighbor, was doorman at the Hotel Gayoso, and could help slip Brother Robert in. Blacks never went to the Peabody at that time. Robert played there. I'm pretty sure that some of those people who slummed were sweet on him, too.

He must have been doing all right in the hotels. He got his pinstripe suit from Eggleston the Tailor on Beale Street. Eggleston made zoot suits for all the young black men. Sister Carrie stayed too busy to sew a suit for him. She didn't have time but to turn in his cuffs and collars when they got worn.

For blacks, Brother Robert played house parties, trying to raise someone's rent money or funeral expenses. He didn't earn much himself. When he got ready for a house party, he would sleep all day in the front room at Sister Carrie's, get up and practice on the front porch, or by the railroad. In the evening he'd load up that eight-eyed range with a fire and boil water for his bath. He emptied out his leather pouch and spread his picks and slides out on the cloverleaf table, and tuned his guitar.

People partied at the Comas house. They'd moved right across Hernando Street from Sister Carrie. The house had a dogtrot, a big long hallway, and he entertained over there. He usually played by himself or with Son. They had certain numbers they performed together, "Salty Dog Blues," "Trouble in Mind," and "Careless Love."

Brother Robert and Son did jokes about Ol' Massa. He wasn't ignorant, he knew some history and had consciousness. Brother Robert and Son had a routine about eating low on the hog, that meant the feet, the ham hock, and chitterlings, while the upper part, the loin and the chops, went to the master. That's what they mean by eating high on the hog. We ate the lights. That's what we call the pig's lungs. They're porous and very light. You make stew out of them.

Brother Robert spoke at times of Haile Selassie, emperor of Ethiopia. He knew about the NAACP and kept up with the Scottsboro Boys case—the people involved had been hoboing to Memphis, just like Brother Robert often did. He followed Paul Robeson's activism and enjoyed Robeson's movie *Show Boat*. He was no dummy, he read the paper. You can hear his awareness of racism in his music. He doesn't want sundown to catch him where he isn't supposed to be. He's telling you something. He knows if you get wrong in the white folks' neighborhood, they'll harm you. White folks are afraid. We were riding out to pick cotton and went up in the wrong yard. We looked up and saw a man with his shotgun pointed right at us, and we backed right out.

The only time I remember Brother Robert having some extra help performing, he brought a woman guitarist, who I think must have been Memphis Minnie. As I remember her, I see a mouth full of gold. That was the in-thing, black people loved that gold.

My sister Charlyne fell and broke her teeth on the brick walkway from our back door. She had a dentist crown them in gold. Sister Carrie had it. Son had it. My father nor my mother had gold. That's why I liked Brother Robert's teeth. He never put gold in his mouth. I used to look at him and think, "beautiful white teeth, that's enough." I always wanted teeth like Brother Robert.

When Brother Robert had his Saturday night house parties, people came dressed to go to church and stayed all night long. I could only stay until my father took me home. One person for certain, Miss B, Bernice, was always there—always at the entertainments, always at Sister Carrie's house or the Comas house—when *he* was there. Brother Robert had a lot of energy. He ended his show with "Take a Little Walk with Me." The people would leave the frolic and go worship next door, to New Light Baptist Church. That's where I was baptized, out back in the deep-water bayou. I've never known Brother Robert to attend church, but he knew every hymn in the book.

I never knew him to be shy, he loved playing for people, and he asked us, "What's your pleasure?" I can imagine him asking the white people in the nice hotels, and I heard him say it myself.

My father's baby sister Aunt Ida visited Chicago several times a year. Their brother William Dodds ran a barbershop on the Southside. That's why Aunt Ida loved

"Sweet Home Chicago." In the lyrics, I think it means he went to Chicago via California. That's how I interpret it. He had family both places, and he's hoboing.

With her toddy in her hand, Aunt Ida would dance on her tippy-toes to "Sweet Home Chicago." No choreography at all, but just tippy-toeing. She was fly and she would dress. She might have on all her cheap jewelry, but you wouldn't be ashamed to take her out anywhere. She never missed the entertainment when Brother Robert was there. She'd come in saying, "Hey, hey!" She took her toddy with honey and hot water and her Old Grand-Dad.

Among my family, "Kind Hearted Woman" was most popular. We all loved "Come on in My Kitchen." I know it has another meaning, but that come on in my kitchen is an old phrase. People used to only have two rooms, one where you slept and one where you sit, and that was the kitchen. That's the main sitting room of the house for us in small houses. His music made me curious. I never knew about Friars Point until I heard him singing.

Brother Robert loved to play for children. Along Hernando Street, beside the railroad track, you had torn down houses with stones and bricks left behind, and he'd sit up there and play nursery rhymes. I'd gather up the Comas children. My friend Gloria Lee Irby, we called her "Baby Lee," lived on Fourth Street, on the other side of Sister Carrie's apartment. Baby Lee and her mother sang gospel, but she'd come listen to Brother Robert, and we'd dance around. I understand he had a broken heart when he lost his baby, but that was grown-up talk, no one told me. Charlyne danced to his music, she was a better dancer than I. She was known as Mary Ruby, because of our Aunt Mary and a friend of our mother's. People always want you to name their children after them.

He played nursery rhymes, "Little Sally Walker," "Mary Had a Little Lamb," "Humpty Dumpty," "Jack and Jill," and "She'll Be Coming Around the Mountain." He told the story of Chicken Little, about how the sky is falling. He did "Mr. Froggie Went to Courting," "Here We Go Round the Mulberry Bush." He kept us entertained making sounds of the train whistle blowing, freight trains chugging, the rooster crowing, crickets, locusts, and frogs you hear at night down South. I'd practiced my reading with him, I recall, back in first grade reading my primer, "Peter Rabbit."

All us children wanted to dance, so he did some blues songs for us. He played up-tempo, I remember well, "Last Fair Deal Gone Down," which the children loved. He'd play that for us about four times and say, "I can't do it anymore." Black folks always call white folks "Captain," like he does in that song, that's to build them up. It's jive, "puttin' on Ol' Massa."

He played a version of "John Henry" where he made the guitar sound like a sledgehammer.

A lot of songs, he'd leave out. That squeeze my lemon, he wouldn't have sung that around children. When he says "if your man gets personal" that means the man wants sex. "If I Had Possession over Judgment Day" is chauvinistic. Couple others are, too.

We heard about barrelhousing, that was a common thing. You're going to be dancing in one of the juke joints and cutting up.

Brother Robert could move, he didn't just sit and play. He could do the shimmy. He could snake hip. His foot would move, he had rhythm. Depending on the song, "Sweet Home Chicago," he wouldn't do a lot of moving. "Terraplane," he'd move a little more. He could rock on some of that stuff. He could shimmy on down. We'd do the Cake Walk, the Charleston, the Black Bottom, the Break Down, and the Mess Around, plus something we called the Levee Camp Stomp.

Brother Robert picked up songs from spiritual sources and he played old-time folk music. From the latter background, he did "John Henry," "Casey Jones," and "John Brown's Body," plus "Loch Lomond," "St. James Infirmary," and "Auld Lang Syne." His spiritual repertoire included "Swing Low Sweet Chariot," "Dry Bones," "Mary Don't You Weep," "When They Ring Them Golden Bells," and "Joshua Fit the Battle of Jericho." Brother Robert knew modern gospel, too, like "Precious Lord (Take My Hand)." He was conversant with W. C. Handy songs, "Memphis Blues," "St. Louis Blues," and "Beale Street Blues."

He even got ideas from the men who sold watermelon and tamales, rolling their carts through town and singing things like, "One for a nickel, two for a dime, would give ya more, but they ain't none a mine."

Today some people want to put Brother Robert on the troubled side. I'm not getting in and saying what didn't happen, because I didn't have him in my pocket. I don't know what he did and didn't do. But I know I've never seen him drunk a day in my life. Sister Carrie took her toddy. Son took his. I know there was drinking, Brother Robert just didn't drink when he played.

He did smoke. During the Great Depression, you smoked what you could. He carried his pouch of Bull Durham and made his own cigarettes. He called those his "roll 'ems."

I've never seen him shoot dice, and I can't say he didn't. People would shoot craps beside the railroad track on Hernando Street every Sunday. I know because our family friend Mr. Martzie Comas did it. When the cops came for a shakedown, Mr. Martzie would come running home out of breath.

Brother Robert was tied up in his music. He never played dozens to my knowing. I can't relate him to any lowdown stuff. To me, he was clean cut. Now, Brother Son, he might have. There were some underworld figures in the neighborhood I know Son associated with.

Down at the corner of Georgia and Wellington was Red Lawrence's pool hall, three blocks from home. The sidewalk would be packed, that was a hangout. You had fistfights, cuts, everything there. Somebody may get shot. The policemen would be running after people because they'd be bootlegging. Red Lawrence and a man named Jim Mulcahy ran the liquor racket. They sold illegal bottled liquor and homemade moonshine, what we called corn liquor. That's where people fought and carried on.

My mother knew about it, she knew about everything. We were well protected. A lot of people didn't like my mother because they thought she felt we were better. Many of the parents were more lenient than my mother. Their children could go places we could never go. Places I went to after my mother died, I would never have gone to as a youngster. The dance hall, Hotel Men's Improvement Club. We couldn't go to those places. At 5 o'clock, we were on our way home. And we thought mother was mean. But she protected us. Not that we didn't make mistakes and get into trouble, but the foundation was laid. We were respected in the community. Not that we were any better than the rest.

We'd watch the police car racing after a black bootlegger in his Cadillac. I didn't know a car could go so fast. They'd go right past our house down Georgia towards 61, and the next street on the right, he's taking Carolina Avenue to the Harahan Bridge, and once he loses the policeman over there, that's it, he'd cross the Mississippi River into Arkansas.

You know if a policeman was behind a black man, the black man would stop. He wouldn't keep going. It was the same man in the same car all the time. I heard the old folks say that was a sham, the policeman pretended he was after the bootlegger. If the policeman wanted to stop him he would have just shot him, because the police were shooting them then just like they are now. No questions asked. Maybe it was in the paper, maybe it wasn't.

One night while everyone slept, the cops came to the

door and started banging. "Open up," I heard them say. This woke my daddy. He opened the door. They were looking for Son, because Son had busted somebody in the lips. All you had to do was mess with Son, he didn't turn the other cheek. Son could be argumentative. Son did drink when he got ready.

He'd been standing outside Red Lawrence's. The cops didn't catch him, though. Son knew not to be at our house when the cops came through.

I can see Brother Robert being around people who drank and played music. When grown folks got together, they did whatever they wanted. But it was Son who gave my father a lot of problems. I never knew of the police banging on the door for Brother Robert.

Jim Mulcahy had a dance hall on Polk Street a few blocks past Red Lawrence's pool hall. Those names were quite prominent around the neighborhood as rough men. But they did a lot for musicians. I heard that Mulcahy brought W. C. Handy from his dance hall to work for Boss Crump's campaign. That's when Handy wrote "Memphis Blues," and started the craze for blues music. We all knew about W. C. Handy since they'd named that park for him on Beale Street. I can imagine Brother Robert worked that same dance hall. You could find it all on a little walk around the neighborhood.

CHAPTER 4

One day, my mother told me, "Carrie wants you to go to Papa Joe's and get some barbecue."

That's where Johnny Rivers, one of Memphis's barbecue kings, sold sandwiches. Brother Robert loved barbecue. We took many a walk to Papa Joe's up on Iowa Avenue between Highway 61 and Fourth Street, or to Johnny Mills, over at Fourth and Beale.

My father went to Sister Carrie's every day, sometimes twice a day. He'd have his second cup of coffee with her. And I think it was makeup, because she grew up feeling upset about him leaving her behind at home. That affected her. As a child, she didn't know why he left.

When I got to Sister Carrie's with the barbecue, I saw my father cutting Brother Robert's hair. All the pots were out, heating water on that stove. That's how Brother Robert took a bath in a cold-water flat. Brother Robert kept himself clinically clean.

He never got into having his hair processed, and my father didn't do new styles. Brother Robert kept his hair neat, using Dixie Peach pomade. He didn't have nappy hair. He could put it anywhere he wanted. He greased Vaseline on his arms and legs to keep his skin from getting cruddy or scaly. Looking up at him, I noticed that his skin had a beautiful reddish undertone.

He was tall, slender, and built like the way women like men, especially black men, to be built. He had the African physique. He didn't have overly broad shoulders, he was high-hipped, had narrow hips.

My father had built a cloverleaf table, stained black, and Brother Robert had his things out on the table—fingerpicks, slides. Some of them looked like thimbles. We'd save beef bones for him, and he'd pick and slide with that some. Brother Robert never wore rings, other than what was ritual, those spread out on the table that he'd play with. I still have that table he played on.

He used to carry them in an empty Bull Durham tobacco sack. That Bull Durham sack would wear out, so my father made him a leather drawstring pouch. It had been emptied out and stood there propped up on that table. His guitar stood, propped up between the clover table leaves. I walked past it. Not thinking, I plucked the strings.

Brother Robert looked at my father, and then he spoke to me about it. He warned me not to touch his guitar. Robert's speaking voice wasn't overly heavy. He had his Southern accent. He would be more polished than country people. But he meant what he said. That's the only time he scolded me. I never did it again.

People have lied about how they used to play Robert Johnson's guitar. *Son* didn't play his guitar. I've never seen anybody play that guitar but Brother Robert. We could go by Son's guitar and rub the strings and Son wouldn't say anything, but Brother Robert was very particular about his things. Robert Johnson didn't allow anybody to touch his guitar. That was his personal object. He has warned me. That paraphernalia he laid on the table? I didn't dare touch it again.

After he cleaned up, we went to Beale Street with Sister Carrie. He carried his guitar with him, and strummed it as we went along. He walked fast with those long legs. He wasn't a big chit-chatter. He may have been different with Son, they were males and I was a child. I had to skip along to keep up.

We all had our photographs taken.

Further up Beale Street at the Palace Theater, we saw Ginger Rogers and Fred Astaire in *Follow the Fleet*. Ginger sang a number called "Let Yourself Go." I thought it catchy, particularly the line "come, let's get together, let the dance floor feel your leather."

The Palace hosted the Beale Street Amateur Night every Tuesday. From yodeling with Brother Robert on those Jimmie Rodgers songs, I got a notion to sing. I decided to go on Amateur Night, and asked Brother Robert to help me.

He had taught me to play a ditty called "Coon Shine Baby" with two fingers on the piano at the Comas house. Now, I wanted him to get me ready to sing "Let Yourself Go." We got me and my steps together. Blacks do not just walk out to the microphone, we always have some type of choreography. The Joe Louis Strut was popular at that time, combined with the dance called truckin'. I got my steps together, practiced, and was ready to make my debut on Amateur Night.

Amateur Night had intense competition. Neighborhood children were on the amateur every Tuesday. Mrs. Price used to dress her two daughters like dolls, they were twins, Thelma Price and Velma Price. They could sing any popular tune. Debra Robinson would sing "That's My Man." Their mothers thought they were going to be stars. Really, many of the acts were professional, but everybody lit out for that three-dollar prize money.

We worked out "Let Yourself Go," there at Sister Carrie's flat. He'd strum and help me with the words.

Amateur Night arrived. I already knew Brother Robert planned to entertain the grown folks, and wouldn't be coming with me. Sister Carrie's friend Miss Essie claimed she'd take me. But when she heard that Brother Robert was entertaining, she changed her mind. She looked me in the face and said she couldn't do it. I cried before her, standing beside the coal box at Sister Carrie's apartment. I boo-hooed. But then, something said, "Go."

I went out looking good, my hair in three plats, with the bows on each plat. Sister Carrie had made me a tiered dress and veil with capped sleeves. I wore little Chinese socks with monograms. I ran all the way up Hernando to Beale Street. Got to the Palace Theater. Mr. Barrasso scooted me up the side steps. A man famous in Memphis named Nat D. Williams always emceed. Jimmie Lunceford led the orchestra that night. He'd started his band in Memphis and become the biggest thing in swing up in New York. My future husband played in Lunceford's band in school. They were playing the theme song, "One O'Clock Jump."

Mr. Barrasso had to tell me to hurry and get on stage, I didn't know what to do. They called me up first or second. I had one foot through the curtain and the band kept telling me to come on out. I was waiting for them to start, but they were waiting on me. I did almost a tap coming out.

I didn't think I was that good, but I must have been moving. I could dance. I didn't get a lot of boos, either. Except from my neighbor, a little boy named Jimmy Crawford. On stage a man called the Lord High Executioner stood with a cap pistol. If the crowd called for it, he'd shoot that pistol and that'd be the end of the routine. I never did hear that gun go off.

At the end of my song, I did that Joe Louis truckin'—I twirled, wound up and scooted, and went out with my forefinger twirling.

I thought my mother wouldn't hear me on the radio, considering her stance against finger-poppin'. She only scolded me for going by myself, because that was a dangerous area. You just didn't go by yourself, but I tell you, I could run, they would have to catch me. I could outrun the boys up to a point. I got myself home safely.

At Sister Carrie's, they all heard me on the radio. Son was there. Brother Robert was there. Whether I did a good job or not, they're going to say they liked it. My mother never went to the entertainments, but said a little birdy told her about me. After I sang "Let Yourself Go," she said she was going to let *me* go. She didn't give me a spanking, though, I think she was kind of proud.

Several people cycled through our house over the years, staying on the other side of the duplex. After Sister Carrie lived there, next came Brother James, he lived there after his wife died. A woman we rented to, Mrs. Appleberry, she died. She was a sanctified lady. She was up in age and disabled. My father would see after her. Evalena and her grandmother lived there. Evalena had a child, Annie, we had the same name. I was older than she. I used to take her to the movies. The daughter was, we called it, "half-white." Sweet little girl, and I wonder sometimes what happened to her. These people came and went at different times.

At school, I sat near a girl named Katie Horton. When school let out, I'd see her brother waiting for her. Later, he became well known as a blues musician, Big Walter Horton. Big Walter was a handsome young man, full face. I can see him now, leaning against the telegram pole, whittling. That's what he always did, waiting for his little sister. They'd go off into the direction of Beale Street, they lived on Fourth.

We had a boy in class who we called "Doughbelly," real name of Eddie Fuquay. Doughbelly used to run with a fellow called "Mickey," whose real name was George Meriwether. They were tight as two peas in a pod. Doughbelly was short, dark-skinned, and plump. Mickey tap-danced, he was excellent, and short as a midget.

I came home from school to my sister's house at 728 Hernando one day, when I was around ten years old, and there was Brother Robert, Big Walter, and Doughbelly. I can see them now, in the kitchen. Doughbelly was trying to blow a harmonica—I saw him watching Big Walter, he was learning. But I wondered what he was doing with the two older men. Though me and Brother Robert were close, we didn't have the relationship where I'd say, "Well, what are you doing here?" I just kept looking and was puzzled. They played "Little Boy Blue," "Sittin' on Top of the World," and "Trouble in Mind."

To see Brother Robert playing with other people surprised me. I knew him to go off to hide in the wrecking yard across from my house to play. He played on the bayou, in the wrecking yard, or over the railroad tracks near Carolina Avenue. Everybody say they knew him, but Brother Robert liked to be by himself. When he wanted to play and practice, he liked to go off alone by the railroad.

His best buddy around Memphis had to be his nephew, Sister Carrie's son Lewis. I knew where to find them, in

The swimming hole Robert Johnson frequented, off Bayou Gayoso. Memphis, 2019. *Photo by Preston Lauterbach*

summer. They had a swimming hole in the bayou, near the wrecking yard, where the water runs a little deeper than it did in front of our house.

I don't know if Lewis traveled with Brother Robert, but in Memphis they were always together, from childhood up. He was born in 1920, so you can see the age difference. Extremely bright. Lewis had a voice. He not only could sing, but could tap. He taught me my first tap dancing steps. Like Brother Robert, Lewis loved Gene Autry, and I can hear him now, teaching all of us "Boots and Saddles." He kept us up on all the latest patriotic songs. He wanted to be a boxer. Joe Louis was in the plan. He turned pro and became a welterweight. He fought as Kid Harris. Not big, not as tall as Brother Robert, but built. He did pressing, worked in a laundry. He and Son used to press Brother Robert's khakis. Sister Carrie taught us to make laundry starch from lard and flour—makes the iron slide right over. It keeps your hair oil from the pillowcase where you rest your head.

Sister Carrie would ask Brother Robert to go and find Lewis, and he wouldn't come back. She'd send me to go find both of them, and they'd be in the bayou swimming. The sun was hot and clothes dried quickly. I'd come back and say I couldn't find them, but she knew I was lying. She knew that Lewis was all right. He was a rough kid.

They want to say that Brother Robert's pinstripe suit was Lewis's, but Brother Robert couldn't wear Lewis's clothes, Lewis was shorter and more broad-shouldered. Brother Robert had narrow shoulders. They had a picture taken together, with Brother Robert in his suit and Lewis in his navy uniform, but Mack McCormick took it from my sister and never gave it back. When she asked him to return it, he sent her an empty envelope.

I palled around with Brother Robert and Lewis. We'd go in the Church of God in Christ temple on Mississippi Boulevard. When those old sisters got out there rockin' and rollin', that was funny to us. My mother would have killed me for cutting up in a church.

We had two ministers in the family, Reverend Cross, my Aunt Ida's husband, who lived nearby, and Brother Granville, Sister Bessie's husband, who lived in Mississippi. Brother Robert had stayed with Brother Granville and Sister Bessie in Mississippi, off and on, throughout the 1930s. Right there at Georgia and Hernando, across the street from home, that was a field, and the sanctified church used to set up a tent and have their revival. Anybody could go in. My mother allowed me to. I heard Rev. Cross preach about the crossroads. He said, "At the crossroads, you must make a decision, determine whether you're going to be Christian and believe." He got that from Jeremiah 6:16, "Stand at the crossroads and look; ask for the ancient paths, ask where the good way is, and walk in it, and you will find rest for your souls. But you said, 'We will not walk in it.'"

I don't know that Brother Robert got his song straight from Rev. Cross, but that's how we were exposed to the idea of the crossroads, listening to the ministers argue in the tent revival over Georgia Avenue. He's probably heard Brother Granville and Rev. Cross saying that. He picked it up.

Hoodoo was in Brother Robert's vocabulary, too. I read where a man who interviewed hoodoo people in Memphis during our time copied down a spell that said,

When you wanta make music easy . . . you take that guitar and that bone then you go to the forks of the road and you sit there and make your music right there . . . that's sellin your soul to the devil.

You know, Baptist people believe in the devil. People talk about the devil and Brother Robert, but he couldn't have lived around Mama Julia without being baptized.

Some folks wanted to believe. There was a man over in Arkansas who'd put a spell on people, but you know he couldn't really put a spell on nobody. If black folks could really cast a spell, they would have done so to their white masters during slavery.

I don't turn my nose up at any religion. I really don't care what you are. Just don't tell me I'm going to hell because I'm not what you are.

CHAPTER 5

I'm still fascinated with trains, because as a little girl all my brothers would take me up to the railroad. The train would stop and put that steam out. I always wanted to go up there. Brother James, Brother Son, and Brother Robert would take me to the railroad to see that train, and when it stopped, to let the hobos off.

One day I heard my brothers singing "Poor Boy a Long Way from Home," and that signaled to me that they planned to depart. I'd love to see Brother Robert and Son run to catch the train. They'd jump on cattle cars, passenger trains. They knew exactly what train was going by Sister Carrie's at Short Hernando Street, where it would slow down at the switch. Both readied to catch the train, with Brother Son leading and Brother Robert behind, loping on those long, lanky legs. Son was shorter and older, Brother Robert let him get on first. They catch hold and pull themselves up, while the train's moving.

The railroad switch at "Short" Hernando Street. Memphis, 2018. *Photo by Preston Lauterbach*

It would be going west towards Arkansas. From there they'd go as far south as Mexico. Son loved the Mexican ladies. He was handsome. I have to say, they must have loved him too. He learned some of the language. I heard them talk about señoritas. Son probably went there several times. It was free to go in and out. Son did hobo. I'm sure he hoboed with Brother Robert and without Brother Robert. And I'm sure Brother Robert hoboed with Son and without Son.

In February 1937, the Mississippi River flooded. Everybody had to leave Arkansas and Mississippi. Refugees from the lowlands filled Memphis. Sister Carrie still lived at 728 Hernando, and all our Delta family came and stayed with us. Everyone slept on pallets, and stayed a long while, except Brother Robert. I can't imagine where he might have been—lucky to be someplace else. In Memphis, the police pulled well-dressed men off of Beale Street and put them to work on the levee, digging mud, piling up sandbags.

That event has stayed with me. During the flood we had people come together from all over. It was like a family reunion. Black folks love to find their kinfolk and pull together in a challenge. In all the time we spent catching up, we never heard about Brother Robert having a son. As sweet as Sister Bessie and Sister Carrie were, they would have loved a son. He would have been welcome. After all, our family embraced Brother Robert even though he was an outside child. We would have embraced his children the same.

I knew very little of Brother Robert's recording career, but around this time Sister Carrie got a letter from him, saying he'd made a record. Sister Carrie and me rushed to Woolworth's on Main Street—that's where black people bought records. They only had one, "Terraplane Blues," and we got it. That's the only one of his records we had and the only one I knew about for many years.

I didn't see Brother Robert again until he came home for Christmas. He did a song about the flood that he called "1937 Waters." He sang it to the tune of an old gospel everyone knew, "Didn't It Rain." It had different words. He could rock on that one.

Christmas was about cooking. Soul food, all the way. Winter vegetables, squash, pumpkins, collard greens. My mother would do three cakes, chocolate, caramel, and coconut. Sweet potato and pumpkin were the main pies. Mama served cake and wine, or her brandy.

I watched my mother make brandy and can still follow her recipe. I can put as much alcohol in it as I want, course you don't want too much, just enough to know it's there. It depends on how much corn you drop in it. I use twelve grains, that's enough. My mother wasn't showing me how to make it, I saw it and I do what I thought she did.

For Christmas dinner, Aunt Ida and Rev. Cross would come over. Mama Julia and Sister Bessie came up and shopped at Schwab's on Beale Street. Got their monkey coats—made out of real monkey fur. Nobody wanted them but black people. People from the country bought monkey.

There weren't gifts at Christmas, we didn't have any money. No cards going around. The only gifts came from the landlady. They may have been cheap or whatever, but we'd been in that house so long, she looked out for us some, at Christmastime.

The next spring, 1938, I turned twelve. I always had picked up a few dimes running errands, shopping for someone, or delivering to Sister Carrie's customers. At that age, I expanded my repertoire. I learned to do hair from a lady named Helen King. You didn't need a license to be a beautician then. She taught me how to use marcel irons and pressing combs. I burned some hair, but I learned. When I became older, a prominent beautician named Madam Hattie Burchett invited me to learn the trade from her for free. I was advised not to do so due to the belief that the smoke from hair processing caused tuberculosis, and we had TB in the family.

While I sometimes did hair at home, there was never enough beauty work to occupy me. To keep making money, I collected throw-outs and sold them. On Front Street, Canale had a fruit stand. I got what they threw out, and when they threw out a lot, there was some good mixed in. I picked out the good apples, bananas, pears. The commerce department, next door to Canale, gave government handouts like margarine. They gave out Clorox in powder form, for sanitary use. It'd eat right through your clothing. Plough chemical company had a factory practically in Sister Carrie's backyard. They'd throw out Epsom salts and jars of Vaseline. In with the broken ones, there'd be some good.

I ran a whole list of errands. I'd pick up sewing supplies for Sister Carrie, go and pay bills at Haverty's furniture store and Goldsmith's department store, shop for groceries, run back and forth between my parents' house and Sister Carrie's, bringing her vegetables our daddy had grown.

If it was at night and I was delivering Sister Carrie's goods, Brother Robert or Son would go with me. Holidays she'd work through the night. Easter, sometime she'd be late delivering. I knew all the neighbors she sewed for.

"Let's go," Brother Robert said. On his long lanky legs, he would walk ahead of me asking, "Which way?" We'd head down the back alleys.

Sometimes I'd be out jumping rope. All Sister Carrie had to do was come to the door and say, "Fats Waller is on." I'd drop that rope and run in. I'd come in and dance. If she had customers, I'd make money dancing for them. I got as much as a quarter put in my hand, a lot of money to a child during the Great Depression.

I could go buy beer as a child, to deliver to my older family members. There was no law against a minor buying beer on an errand. I'd go to Pete's on the corner of Georgia, east side of Fourth Street. Pete served whites and blacks. Pete's was segregated, clear-cut, whites on one side, blacks on the other. We were on the east side, and whites came in on the west side. The front faced Georgia Avenue and when you walked in and looked back, he had the big Seeburg in the corner, there it stood. I don't know of any problem blacks had there. I bought Falstaff, Goldcrest 51, Pabst Blue Ribbon. I could go and buy the big bottle, the quart. Sister Carrie drank beer, though not every day. Son drank beer.

We would save the tops, Baby Lee and I, and other children would turn them over and try to guess which brand it was. I collected the tops, so I always won, I knew the shape and how each top looked.

I could go get cigarettes. Sister Carrie smoked Camels, Chesterfields, and the Bull Durham roll 'ems when money had got tight.

Sister Carrie left the apartment at 728 Hernando when the rent got high. After that, she lived at 337 St. Paul Avenue, first house from the corner, next door to Kerrigan's fish market. There were shacks all around.

She still had the radio, so there was no doubt about where the family would gather to listen to the big fight, Max Schmeling versus Joe Louis. I'll never forget the date, June 22, 1938. That was going to be a festive night. With everyone up from Mississippi, we'd have us all together to celebrate Brother Robert's birthday. When Sister Carrie had a house party, she'd fill up a coal bin with ice and beer. We picked up a big load of beer bottles for that fight.

Joe Louis was a hero to all. Brother Robert loved boxing above all sports, and Joe Louis was his favorite athlete by far. This fight with Schmeling was a rematch. Although Louis was the champ, he'd lost his last bout against Schmeling. Plus, everyone on both sides saw extra importance in the race issue. Schmeling had Hitler pulling for him. Joe Louis had every black person in America. An article in the *Memphis Press-Scimitar*, the paper my father read every day, billed the fight as the "Nazi from the Black Forest" against "the negro from the American cottonfields."

Mama Julia came up from Mississippi to listen to the fight, with Mr. Willis. They caught a ride with a friend named Doc Belton. I don't know, but I really think he was a boyfriend of Sister Carrie's. He'd come up and get her and bring her down to Robinsonville and take her back. I can't say, but they were close. He was Brother Robert's transportation back and forth. Reliable. He had a small truck. Doc was young, along with Sister Carrie. I know he was at her beck and call.

Brother Robert rode with them to come to the party. You should have seen him in his white sharkskin suit, Panama hat, and patent leather shoes. He was razor sharp when he dressed. Son, Sister Carrie, my father, and Lewis all were there, as was the Comas family.

We had barbecue and people brought pies. We had the big dinner, everything except chitterlings. We had Brother Robert's favorite dishes, candied yams, fried pumpkin. In the South, we always had a tossed salad. My father grew lettuce and onions out front of our house, so we always had a fresh salad.

The fight began at eight in the evening. It didn't last long. Brother Robert kicked his lanky legs up when Joe Louis knocked out Schmeling in the first. It made all of us black folks happy. We could hear the whole street cheering.

I didn't stay under the radio afterwards. That gave my sister Charlyne and me a time as young children to run and get out of sight, go as far as we wanted to go away from the ol' folks. We'd be on the street going where we wanted to go while they'd be shoutin' and carryin' on. Everybody on the street had the radio on. Everyone's lights were on, they were barbecuing. It really was a heyday.

That night, Brother Robert performed "Terraplane," "Sweet Home Chicago," "Kind Hearted Woman," he and Son did "44 Blues." My father took me home, because

Location of Sister Carrie's apartment, St. Paul Avenue, Memphis, where Robert Johnson performed last on June 22, 1938, as it appeared eighty years later. *Photo by Preston Lauterbach*

Brother Robert was going to play all night. I don't know much else about Brother Robert's performance. Other than it was the last time he played in Memphis.

That night of the big fight was the last time I saw him. I wish you could have seen him jump for joy in his white suit. It looked like his legs about went up to the ceiling.

He left the next morning. The people who brought him up, Doc Belton and his mother Mrs. Belton, they were ready to get back on the farm. Brother Robert rode off with them. I don't know if he stayed in Robinsonville or went straight away to Greenwood, where he died.

The telegram came to Sister Carrie on St. Paul Avenue. I don't know who sent it. I wasn't there when it came. Sister Carrie went to pieces. I think she was closer to Brother Robert than anyone else in the family. Everyone was in shock. He was dead two weeks before we knew. It felt awful. It was hard to believe because he had just left. I was sad, but as a child, you don't really know what death is. We weren't going to sing Jimmie Rodgers together, ever again, or sing "John Henry" together any more. You don't realize that as a child. I didn't know we weren't going to see his feet rockin' anymore, or watch his slides going up and down the guitar strings.

Sister Carrie, Mama Julia, Sister Bessie, Brother Granville, and Mr. Willis all went to Greenwood to claim the body, but it was too late. He was already in the ground. They buried Brother Robert before family could get to him. They were told, "We buried him because the body was decomposing."

We don't know what he died of. Brother Robert was young and healthy. I've heard some speculation that he died of syphilis. There are signs when a person has syphilis. They were sending black folks out to get penicillin back then, so I don't think that was it. Sister Carrie heard a story about him being poisoned. She said he drank it in beer, and he knew at the first sip. He lingered for a week.

If those people in Greenwood were his friends, why didn't we ever hear from them? If Honeyboy Edwards was as close to Brother Robert as he's stated, Honeyboy could have found out where we were. After Brother Robert died, friends from Beale Street came to offer condolences, for as long as three years after they'd learned he passed. That's why I don't believe Brother Robert was crawling around like a dog. Black people will tell white people anything to get a dollar. I'm just telling what I know.

After he died, a few of his things came to us: his guitar—which Son later got hold of and pawned—and a scrap of paper. We were told it was Brother Robert's death-bed confession. The family calls it his testimony. He wrote in beautiful cursive with green ink. The message says:

> Jesus of Nazareth, king of Jerusalem, I know that my Redeemer liveth and that He Will call me from the Grave

I believe that came true. He's had a life after death longer than his life on earth.

He's been gone so long, over eighty years. I think of saying goodbye to him. Walking with him to Third Street, Highway 61, where he'd hitch a ride across the Harahan Bridge, going over the Mississippi River. I still think of how it felt to hug him. He put his skinny arms around me. His clothes felt starched and pressed. His face felt smooth. He smelled like cigarettes and Dixie Peach.

II

The Afterlife of
Robert Johnson

CHAPTER 6

Brother Robert's death began a time of pain for our family. Within four years, both of my parents were dead, Sister Carrie and Lewis had left Memphis, and my sister Charlyne and myself were broken apart. I went through this all before I reached the age of sixteen.

My father didn't have a lot to tell girls, but he taught me every tool he had. I followed him around and helped with his work. I know he worked mostly for whites, and blacks could hardly pay him. My father had cancer, before that was well understood or talked about. He worked up until two weeks before he died. He was on our roof fixing a leak, and he had a fall. He'd gotten weak, and that put him to bed for good. He never was a lay-around person, always energetic and on the move.

We still lived in the duplex at the rear of 285 Georgia Avenue. My father was ailing in one half of the duplex, and since it was Thanksgiving, we were over on the other side cooking a wild rabbit. My older sister Charlyne and I had to watch the rabbit because my mother stayed with my father. I would come in and speak to him. He did know that he was dying, I was looking at his mouth when he said, "This is the end." I never will forget. He didn't appear to be afraid. I didn't see the last breath go.

He passed on Thanksgiving Day, November 28, 1940. I hope he's remembered as Robert Johnson's first guitar teacher.

My mother, sister, and me went to live with the Comas family. Brother Pete took us all in. He was a very kind man. He and my father had grown up together. In addition to his son, son's wife, and their children, it was a crowded house. We didn't have much room to bring anything from the old house, but put my father's trunk in the hallway, where it sat for a couple of years.

My mother still worked hard. She didn't go back to picking cotton, she worked at the Kelly home, helping our white friends. She had high blood pressure and a kidney problem, and doctors didn't know how to treat it.

I went over to see my mother at the hospital when she took ill. This was only a year and a half after my father passed. She wanted to know why everything was so dark in there. I didn't realize she had lost her eyesight.

I was fifteen when my mother died. My friend Baby Lee's mother, Mrs. Irby, made my mother's shroud from white fabric I picked out at Goldsmith's. She told me you don't bury a woman my mother's age in white, but Mrs. Irby made the shroud anyhow.

It was in March 1942, with the funeral held at New Light Baptist Church, next door to the Comas house. There was no room next to my father, so she's buried at Rose Hill Cemetery, diagonally across from where my father is buried at Mt. Carmel. He had a headstone, but it's worn away, and my mother never did have one. In 2015, I visited Memphis to find the gravesites, but the cemetery was so poorly maintained, nothing could be found.

Without my parents to take care of me, making a living became my number one thing to do. I loved school and had perfect attendance, but I had to drop out. The Comas family couldn't take care of me and my sister Charlyne with all the children they had. I never wanted to break from my sister, but we had to go our separate ways and stay with different family friends.

Mrs. Smith, who ran the café where my mother had worked, took in my sister Charlyne. A lady named Willie Thompson took me in, right across the street from the Comas place. We had always called Mrs. Thompson "Ma." Her husband was Garfield Thompson, who worked at Hotel Gayoso, and used to let Brother Robert in the back door. We called him "Pops."

Ma wanted my mother's iron pans and skillets. My mother had a skillet big enough for two chickens, so I brought those. I got my family photographs out of my father's trunk.

Brother Robert's old girlfriend, Miss B, took over when my mother died. She was a big sister, always that person giving advice. She was a social worker. She had a

Studebaker with the rumble seat, we used to ride in the back. Bernice West, she later married a man named Bradley and she became Bernice West Bradley. Bernice moved to Washington, DC.

I got out there and went to work. I checked fur coats and hats at the Variety Club. I worked at Britling's Cafeteria. They fired me for being sassy. They waited until the end of my shift to tell me my sister had gotten sick and been taken to the hospital. I told them what I thought about that.

After Britling's, I was a short-order cook, working at Beer Barrel Polka across from the Greyhound station on Calhoun at Second Street. Brother Robert's shoeshine man, a one-legged fellow named Britt, had his stand right there. The Polish man who ran Beer Barrel Polka used to dance every night at eight o'clock with a mug of beer on his head, and he never spilled a drop.

I got fired from there for taking too long washing the greens. They had bugs on them. My mother had taught me to move greens from water to water, soaking away all the dirt, worms, and that white mess on the back of the leaves. You have to take a cloth and wipe them off. I did all that and the man told me I took too long. That's why I don't eat greens out.

After living apart for a year or two, my sister and I decided to move in together on Pontotoc Avenue. Charlyne was always a bookworm, reading, reading, reading. Very bright. She was valedictorian and a champion speller. She

took Latin. She didn't have much use for it though, working at the Railroad Grill.

After that, I answered an ad in the paper to get a job
with Mrs. Gerber. When you were black you got a social security card early, because they expect you to become a maid.
When you start school, they put you in domestic sciences.
You learn every part of the cow from the filet mignon to the
oxtail. This is the way it is, because you are programmed
to become somebody's maid. A lot of black folks rather do
other things than work in white folks' kitchens. That was a
stigma. Girls were sent to college to keep them out of the
white folks' kitchen. Without my parents to take care of
me, I went to work in the house of Mrs. Gerber.

I had to catch the bus on Main Street and ride it up
Poplar Avenue to Chickasaw Gardens. She lived at 99
Cherokee Drive. I came in from a back road through her
gate and into the yard. Mrs. Gerber had a yardman, an
upstairs maid, and cook. Her husband was dead, and they
had a son, twelve years old. I was downstairs maid and assisted with dinner.

Mrs. Gerber was as nice to me as any person ever has
been. But she was racist as hell. She fed me well. She said,
"You can have anything you want as long as you don't
waste the food." She paid eight dollars a week, and that
was uncommon for my age, seventeen. This was as much
or a little more than some of the older maids earned.

Mrs. Gerber knew I liked to dress, and she gave me a
Russian sable stole that went all the way to the knee. She

used to call me in to the guests to show them my figure, though I don't know why.

I left there and got a war job, in North Memphis, at a big manufacturing plant called Burton and Dixie. We made cotton batting for the Jeeps during the war. I had to quit when the boys came back from the war, veterans got first choice of jobs.

Sister Carrie had left Memphis not long after Brother Robert died. The navy stationed her son Lewis at Annapolis, Maryland, and Sister Carrie moved there to be near him. She met an oysterman named Sanky Thompson, they married, and built a home in Churchton, Maryland. When my sister moved to Maryland, she shipped Brother Robert's guitar to her mother's house in Mississippi. Son could sweet-talk you out of anything. He talked Sister Carrie into giving him the guitar, so she told Mama Julia he could get it. That's how it was pawned and lost. Son couldn't afford to get it out. Brother Robert's guitar might still be somewhere in Memphis. I still have the cedar chest it used to be in.

Mama Julia came to stay with Sister Carrie twice. First with Mr. Willis. He didn't like Maryland and went back to Robinsonville, Mississippi. Mama Julia felt guilty about letting him go and went back and stayed with him until he died. Mr. Willis passed on May 7, 1947. Their last address is now under a casino, and the church where Mr. Willis was buried no longer exists. After he died, Mama Julia came back and stayed with Sister Carrie. I know Mama Julia worked the garden, Sister Carrie had a big back yard.

Mama Julia used to wash outdoors. Sister Carrie got a washing machine, but Mama Julia couldn't stand it. You put the water in it and wash, but Mama Julia had her rub board outside. I took photographs of that when I was selling the house. The tubs were there as Mama Julia left them.

Finally, I left Memphis for good in 1947 when I reached the age of twenty-one. I left Memphis by train. Sister Carrie had wanted me to come up for a long time. Brother Sanky picked me up at the station.

I gave my sister Charlyne the furniture in our house. She wasn't as close to Sister Carrie as I was, and she was older and wanted to live independently. She remained in Memphis. I kept my father's old trunk, and Sister Carrie told me how to ship my things up. I even shipped up her old .32 pistol. It had no firing pin and the handle was hollow. It barely was a gun anymore.

I went up there to Maryland and stayed with Sister Carrie and Sanky. I have nothing but good memories of Brother Sanky. He worked hard, like Mr. Willis. He had his faults, liked his drink, but he could hold his liquor. He was a strong man, pulling up those tongs of oysters by the bushel. Sanky took me out on his boat, and a storm came up. I told the Lord, if you let me see the sun shine on the Chesapeake again, I'll never get on a boat no more. And I never did.

Sister Carrie and Brother Sanky only had two bedrooms in their house. I wanted to leave anyway, because it's out in the country. You had to walk everywhere you went, and there was nothing to do. For me, coming from the city, that was out. I did door-to-door sales and made good money. I sold hose, socks, Christmas cards, stockings.

Brother Sanky was an independent man, and wouldn't take a nickel from me. I saved my money.

When Mama Julia came up to live with Sister Carrie, I decided to go to Washington, DC. I had never been before, but I'm adventurous. I've always had confidence in myself. Sister Carrie didn't want me to go, but I didn't like that country life. I didn't have anything in common with the people out there. Neither did Sister Carrie, because she was sort of an outcast there. It's not like in the South where people take you in. You never become close. People didn't have the relationships like we had in Memphis.

I took a bus, got to DC, and took a job working at a department store cafeteria, bussing dishes. The department store where I worked was segregated, and I couldn't eat where I worked. I learned quickly that the South holds no monopoly on racism. People say it's covert or it's this or that, no, it's the same. People can't see it. Martin Luther King said, "You can ride in the front of the bus, but what difference does it make when you don't have bus fare?" Don't expect black people to tell you the truth, because they don't. But if you don't tell whites how things really are, they'll never know. In our nation's capital, it took me my entire first lunch hour to find someplace to serve me a meal. It must be known that there is only one region in the United States, you're either up South or down South.

I found a place to live right away in Northwest, off of U Street, near the Howard Theater and Howard University.

There was a lady who rented out rooms. She told me, "I have a man living here who's from Memphis, too." Lo and behold, late that evening, I met Hugh Anderson. I knew of him from his playing with Jimmie Lunceford's orchestra. We soon started courting.

I knew Miss B, our old friend from Memphis, had moved to DC. We had been in touch, Sister Carrie had her over for dinner in Maryland. I stayed in contact with her. As I got to know Hugh very well over the next couple of months, she was happy for me.

I had friends around. Alma, Miss B's adopted daughter, came up and got her nursing degree from Howard University. I told them that Hugh and I planned to get married. Within three months of meeting, Hugh and I got married in Miss B's living room by her pastor.

We had so much in common. The fact that he's a scientist and I just had a GED didn't matter. One of my teachers at UDC had a husband working at the same plant where my husband worked. She couldn't figure out how I had this man, a scientist, but didn't even have a college degree. DC people are very class-conscious and color-conscious. My husband's fair and I'm dark. That doesn't work in DC.

We saw black people passing for white, but we never said anything, that's their business, if they want to go. As blacks, if you had a Southern accent, you had to take speech to help you get rid of it if you planned to go into teaching as I did.

My husband worked with Dr. Charles Drew in 1949 at Howard University. I went to the lab, my husband wanted me to meet Dr. Drew. They had little chicks all over the lab. I never thought to ask my husband, "What do the chicks have to do with the blood?" Dr. Drew established blood banks during World War II.

From my first job, I advanced as a clerk. I worked for the Commerce Department, the Air Force, and later for the Library of Congress. Hugh and I had two daughters. First Hughia July 17, 1949, and next came Sheila, November 13, 1951. I left my job to raise our girls and to continue my education.

Mama Julia passed on April 22, 1949. She had a heart attack. She's buried in a small cemetery in Anne Arundel County, Maryland. Later I tried to move her grave from wet ground, but it's lost. We wouldn't even be able to find her body because the graves are under flood waters.

Brother Son died of a cerebral hemorrhage in 1961 at age sixty-three. He's buried in Tunica County, Mississippi. I've searched for his grave, but couldn't find a marker.

I still had Sister Carrie and Sister Bessie nearby. Whenever we got together over the years around the time of Brother Robert's birthday, we always had the food that he liked, fried pumpkin. He liked spaghetti, we thought we were cooking Italian, but much later, after I started eating out, I realized we had really made black folks' spaghetti. We always remembered Brother Robert through the things he enjoyed.

CHAPTER 7

My family left Washington, DC, after I got my bachelor's degree from District of Columbia Teachers College, known now as UDC. My husband worked at a lab in Cambridge, Massachusetts, doing food science. I started teaching and eventually moved to Boston and taught in the public schools.

I taught mostly Caucasian males. They thought they'd run me out, but when my students left me they had a new idea about black people as teachers. One of my students said, "Mrs. Anderson, you got your boots on." I said, "Yeah, laced all the way up to the hip." Another young man asked me my qualifications. I told him everything I'd done from short order cook, on up. He said, "I'll never ask for your qualifications again."

Sometime in the late '60s, I read an article in *Ladies Home Journal* about the British boys who were playing American rock 'n' roll. One of them said he was inspired by the music of bluesman Robert Johnson. I wondered, "Are they talking about my Robert Johnson?" I couldn't think of how they knew about him.

Sister Carrie and Sister Bessie and I spoke of him. Sister Carrie's verbose, just like I am. We'd get on the phone and talk for hours. Brother Robert came to me, often, in my mind. We talked about his one record we had. I said, "Sister Carrie, when Brother Robert did the 'Terraplane Blues,' he wasn't talking about a car." She said, "No, baby." We both admitted we never saw him drive—that song was about a woman. He really stripped it down. When I was younger, I wasn't smart enough to follow that.

Sister Carrie and I also wrote letters back and forth, and I've kept all she sent me. The letters show what she went through and tell her side of a story that no one really knows—how my family lost Brother Robert again.

Just like it used to be back in Memphis, Sister Carrie was the glue that held the family together. Only now, everyone had trouble. Sister Carrie's husband Sanky had passed in 1954, leaving her in that house in the country in Maryland. She lived on a little Social Security and with the help of social services, on a fixed income of less than $200 per month.

Sister Bessie was towards the end of her life. Sister Bessie and Brother Granville had moved to Maryland to be near Sister Carrie, and they settled in Laurel, where Brother Granville found a flock he could preach to. He finally became a real minister. They built a little shed house. Brother Granville had died, and when Sister Bessie got sick, she moved to Churchton to stay with Sister Carrie. Sister Carrie wrote to me in March of 1973 to tell me, "Bessie looks well better than I have seen her in some time, she eats well, but her mind isn't too stable at times, she has lost interest in caring for herself . . . I will do for her as long as I can, she is still a sweet sister, she loves you very much."

Sister Carrie tried to keep Sister Bessie moving. "We went to a meeting last nite at the social services bldg . . . seems that Nixson wants to take what little help we are getting away." She told me how she'd become president of the Forever Young Club and started leading a sewing circle, "So it isn't so loansome around here any more like it uster be . . ."

Sister Carrie had to keep herself moving, too. Sister Bessie was in her early eighties, and Sister Carrie was about ten years younger. She talked about how she had to give Sister Bessie her bath and a rub down. "That will help some, but she doesn't want to stir around because it hurts. Well, if I give over to hurt, I would sit all day to, but I find it better to move because I hurt some where all the same."

Sister Bessie's condition grew worse, but Sister Carrie kept her sense of humor. "Anne, she doesn't look right to me. She is getting so seanile . . . the Dr says get her up and I do but it takes two to three hours to get the job done . . . I make her laugh, I say if I don't wash Possible you will run everyone away, I say I have to wash my Possible every day too. She will laugh and say I never heard that word Possible before. I told her Lucille calls it fish box—so much for that."

Sister Carrie stayed tough because so many counted on her. Sister Carrie's son Lewis was in and out of the house. "Hoping he will get on his feet once more and take care of himself," she told me.

Sister Carrie took care of Lewis's son, named Robert. Lewis did love that boy. He called him "Barbed-Wire."

My sister Charlyne had a nervous breakdown and was in and out of the hospital. There'd always been trouble and tension along with the love of my sister Charlyne. Sister Carrie remembered us all so well and understood us. "I love her yes," Sister Carrie wrote about Charlyne, "but you no your self, Anne, every since she found out that we wasn't whole sisters she acted different . . ."

Still, Sister Carrie took in Charlyne's teenaged daughter when Charlyne had to go away. That girl gave Sister Carrie and Sister Bessie no end of trouble. Sister Carrie wrote,

She is doing very well in school but she is Hell on wheels at home, she makes up songs and sangs what she wants to say about having two no good aunts . . . she shoved me back against the door, I grabbed her by the coat collar and held on about five minutes until I got to the wash basin and popped her side the head. She let go by that time. I was so out of breath I could have had a heart attack or stroke . . . I don't want to knock her mouth and go to jail . . . I have lived this long and haven't been to jail, but if she hits Bessie, that's where you can write me because I'll give her all I have got.

Sister Carrie told Charlyne, "She got some of that from you, because when you was little you would crawl up to the bench when Mrs. Mollie was doing the wash and do the shimmie she wobble, get the dish cloth off the table and try to wash between your legs, and tell Aunt Ida she was good for nothing but eating and shitting." Charlyne had to laugh.

No matter what Sister Carrie went through, she knew who she was and felt pride in herself. "In the flesh I'm as good as any woman," she wrote. About Caucasians, she thought, ". . . so far as the white crackers, I go along with them so far as I no that most of them hate to see Negroes come up as far as they has and I do hope the younger generation will have it better. It has been hard for us all our lives. They want us to just keep our heads above water . . . they put on a act, and I put on one just to get what I want." It's a telling thought, knowing what else was happening.

Sister Bessie died on January 6, 1974. My mother had said long ago Sister Bessie was the prettiest of Mama Julia's daughters. Sister Bessie stayed looking young a long time. Even in her casket, she was rosy as a peach. She's buried in a small cemetery in Deale, Maryland, where Mama Julia and Brother Sanky were laid to rest.

A couple months later, Sister Carrie wrote to me. "Now I will give you a little good news. It was a fellow here yesterday . . . he formerly lived in California but has lived three years in Memphis. He had been down around Hazlehurst . . . [and] Robinsonville, Commerce, Miss. And found out about Bro Robert and his records . . . In Commerce, Miss [he] found out I was in Maryland . . . came to DC and through the phone company found my phone number . . ."

This is how I learned about Steve LaVere. He was a young white man, who'd been going around Mississippi asking questions about Robert Johnson. People down there who knew the family led him to Sister Carrie. I found out later, LaVere wasn't the first to search for Brother Robert and find Sister Carrie.

A man named Mack McCormick had been to see Sister Carrie, and she'd given McCormick a photograph of Brother Robert with her son, Lewis. Later we learned that Sister Bessie had given McCormick other family photographs that were never returned. That was the last any of us ever saw of McCormick.

Steve LaVere was about to become a fixture in our lives for years to come. What happened to my family must be the greatest example of a white man stealing a black man's soul. Steve LaVere never knew Brother Robert. He was born after Brother Robert died. He had no connection to Brother Robert's family.

People say Steve LaVere made Robert Johnson a legend. No. Steve LaVere didn't tell Eric Clapton about Robert Johnson. He didn't tell Led Zeppelin or the Rolling Stones. Musicians already knew Brother Robert's work before LaVere got into the picture. That's the whole reason LaVere got involved. Those big artists had covered Brother Robert's songs that nobody had copyrighted.

Brother Robert was already a goldmine fifteen years before he won a Grammy. Steve LaVere caught on before anyone else, and we never caught up to him.

Back when Mack McCormick and Steve LaVere came to Sister Carrie, she couldn't believe it, because we didn't know anyone else knew about Brother Robert. She thought LaVere was the cat's meow but later found out he was not the dog's bow wow! At first, he approached Sister Carrie only with the idea of writing a book about Brother Robert. Same as Mack McCormick, he said he'd write Brother Robert's biography and help Sister Carrie get Brother Robert's royalties. I spent the next several years trying to help Sister Carrie get what she was entitled to—money generated by Brother Robert's music. She got nothing—even though she was Brother Robert's only known living heir—and LaVere got it all.

Sister Carrie was minding her own business when these men got in touch with her. She didn't seek out McCormick, LaVere, or any other attention for Brother Robert. With people like them, Sister Carrie was at a disadvantage because she didn't know the value of Brother Robert. We didn't know he was famous. The Rolling Stones, Led Zeppelin, and Eric Clapton, I knew they existed, but I didn't know they were doing Robert Johnson songs.

In late April 1974, Sister Carrie wrote me, "Well Anne I had a call from the guy in Memphis, he is suppose to come up soon so that we could get together with Bro Robert's songs. He said he found that someone had stolen some of them. He said so we could go to a lawyer and get thangs straight, he suggested D.C. I told him that I had a lawyer in Annapolis, what was wrong about going to my lawyer . . . So he said perfect . . ."

Sister Carrie needed something good to happen for her, and hoped LaVere could be it.

CHAPTER 8

During this time my husband was job-hunting around Illinois, and I was staying with our daughter Sheila and our grandson in Massachusetts. I had my teaching job and I couldn't rush to help Sister Carrie.

At first, I saw no reason to. She felt satisfied with the way LaVere handled their business. She sent me a letter in late September of 1974, though, telling me something had gone wrong. You can see her frustration. She sent me a small photograph she had showing Brother Robert with a cigarette in his mouth, and the paper containing his dying words. She had already loaned LaVere the photograph that was made of Brother Robert in his pinstripe suit at Hooks Brothers on Beale Street. She wanted me to copy the cigarette photo for LaVere. She explained:

I don't intend to let Steve LaVere have the original ever, he has suckered me enough with his Lies. So if I don't get any thang, I will be back where I started, because he has me over a barrel . . . I will send the copy of the verse from the bible and the picture. If he can get any money from the big picture he can do the same with the rest of the stuff. I was just dumb to the whole thang till I got into it, then I suspected him of being a crook and found out he had collected the 500 . . . I no I am licked, but as you say I don't have money to fight back but I won't sign for him to have the pictures. Even after I am gone, if no one wants them I'll have them put in the ground with me . . . if I was able and was not 71 years old I would fight him like a Mad Dog for taking me for one thing and doing another . . . I haven't signed any papers yet . . .

The "500" she mentioned had come to LaVere from a record company that wanted to produce a new collection of Brother Robert's music. She hadn't known anything about the new record at the time LaVere contacted her. He had only mentioned writing a book. LaVere sent her $300 for providing him biographical information about Brother Robert and her family photos—two of Brother Robert, one of Brother Son and his wife, one of Mama Julia, and one of our father—to use in what LaVere called "The Complete Robert Johnson." Once she cashed that check, LaVere felt like he owned it all.

Although Sister Bessie had gone on, Sister Carrie worried about her son Lewis, Brother Robert's good buddy. In the middle of all the upheaval with LaVere, she wrote me, "Anne, if they don't get him away where he can get some kind of care and away from that wine. That's the first thang he wants when he wakes up in the morning. I have done a mother's part and over so that all I can do is pray for him . . . I no that your arms isn't long enough to reach me, but I do feel that you care." She still had family stress.

Sister Carrie told her lawyer about LaVere and the book about Brother Robert, and sent the lawyer a letter, saying, "I am in hopes you will protect me."

Soon, she began to tell me how her lawyer didn't respect her. He'd talk to Steve LaVere without telling her what they were talking about. They drew up a contract and the lawyer told Sister Carrie, "You wouldn't understand it if I gave it to you." He advised her to sign. It's clear in her letters from this time that she was trying to understand the process, they just wouldn't allow her in.

People talk about Brother Robert selling *his* soul. This was the real Robert Johnson deal with the devil. Sister Carrie didn't trust LaVere, but she had no one else who could help her find Brother Robert's earnings. So she signed a contract with him on November 20, 1974.

It is agreed by the parties hereto that Mrs. Thompson hereby transfers to LaVere all of her right, title and interest, including all common law and statutory copyrights, in and to the musical works and recordings of Robert L. Johnson; a photograph of Robert L. Johnson taken by Hooks Brothers Photography in Memphis, Tennessee . . . a small

photograph of Johnson with a guitar, and a note written by Johnson . . . another photograph of Johnson and
Mrs. Thompson's son . . . it being understood that Mrs.
Thompson, her heirs and assigns will maintain possession
of the originals of the above-mentioned photographs.

. . . LaVere hereby agrees . . . to take all steps required
to register and protect the statutory copyright or other like
interest in such items . . . LaVere agrees to pay unto Mrs.
Thompson in consideration . . . fifty percent of all royalties
as collected by him, said sum to be paid quarterly.

Over the next year, things began to fall apart. Sister
Carrie wasn't treated fairly, and she asked for my help.
LaVere communicated only with her lawyer, and Sister
Carrie never heard from anyone. She thought that I knew
what to do, because I was educated, but really, I didn't
know diddley. I didn't get involved until things got messy.
All I could think to do was find out what LaVere had been
up to.

I drove down from Boston to Maryland and tried to
get Sister Carrie's legal papers from the lawyer's office. His
secretary got everything for me. He never would introduce
himself, just stood at the head of the stairs as she went to
the files. So now I'm that Yankee Negro who comes down
to make everything hard.

We got copies of letters between Steve LaVere and
Sister Carrie's lawyer, Mr. Stevens. The first thing we noticed was that LaVere had kept Sister Carrie in the dark

Sister Carrie was the backbone of the family. She reared Brother Robert and fought for many years for the control of his estate. *Author's collection*

This is Brother Son with his wife, Sadie. Brother Robert and Brother Son hoboed together and performed music together. *Author's collection*

My father's baby sister Ida loved for Brother Robert to sing "Sweet Home Chicago," and she'd dance on her tippy toes. *Author's collection*

Brother Granville, my sister Bessie's husband, used to argue with other ministers about the crossroads. Brother Robert lived with them in his late teens. *Author's collection*

Some say Brother Robert was illiterate, but you can see he had beautiful handwriting. He sent this to Sister Carrie when he was recording in Dallas. *Author's collection*

Sister Carrie's restaurant in Bunker Hill, South Memphis, where Brother Robert probably performed. *Author's collection*

Sister Carrie had this taken on Beale Street in Memphis. She was a pretty woman and a fly dresser. *Author's collection*

Sister Bessie kept Brother Robert at her home in Mississippi. My mother always said Bessie was the prettiest of Mama Julia's daughters. *Author's collection*

These are two of my father's siblings, Uncle Will and Aunt Ida. *Author's collection*

Not long after Brother Robert died, Sister Carrie moved to Annapolis, Maryland, and married an oysterman named Sanky Thompson. *Author's collection*

In the middle is Brother Sanky, and second from the left is Sister Carrie, outside their home in Churchton, Maryland. *Author's collection*

That's me and Sister Carrie at her house. I stayed with Sister Carrie after I left Memphis in 1947. *Author's collection*

Here I am visiting down in Mississippi in my younger days. *Author's collection*

This is the little old lady Steve LaVere took to the cleaners, and my Sister Carrie on the right. *Author's collection*

You can see the beautiful personality of my daughter Hughia. I dedicate this book to her and to Sister Carrie. *Author's collection*

about a Robert Johnson record he was producing. She only knew about him writing a book. Two months after he got Sister Carrie to sign that contract, LaVere told Mr. Stevens, "The record should have been out by now—a reporter in Chicago just last week told me that he received test pressings about 2 months ago!"

It looked like LaVere had already started to produce the record before he'd gotten Sister Carrie's approval. She had no idea the record project was that far along. She felt like all of this was happening without her knowledge or input. LaVere pushed to have her sign another contract, with CBS Records. "As soon as that aspect is tied up I shall begin investigation into song copyrights and the collection of artist and composer royalties," he claimed.

LaVere and the record company ran into trouble from Mack McCormick, the white record collector who met Sister Carrie before LaVere. She had signed a piece of paper McCormick typed up, allowing McCormick to write a biography of Brother Robert. That document said that McCormick had offered to help collect Brother Robert's royalties on Sister Carrie's behalf. Now McCormick used his little piece of paper to threaten legal action against the record company. LaVere wrote to Sister Carrie's attorney, saying, "I would like to have [Carrie] revoke her permission and withdraw her request regarding the [McCormick] biography [of Robert Johnson] as well as to request that he make no attempts at royalty collection. As you can understand, one book on the subject would be more beneficial to her than two, one of which will be very inferior, and two people attempting royalty collections would be very confusing to a publisher or record company."

Meanwhile, LaVere was trying to get the record company to go ahead with the release. He wrote Sister Carrie in May of 1975, "I have not sent you any records or book. Let me explain: CBS and I are still in contract finalization stages. (They are unbelievably slow with this project—much to my great surprise!) But I expect a release sometime this summer. Also, MacMillan has expressed a sincere desire to publish my manuscript (when it is completed) . . . and have promised me a written commitment and contract this June . . . Please be patient and I'm sure I'll do you proud."

LaVere never got a contract from MacMillan and never published a book about Robert Johnson anyway. That whole story was just a fraud.

LaVere went to New York to work on the Robert Johnson record, and he did send Sister Carrie $600 out of $2,500 he'd made. LaVere calculated that amount himself and left it to Sister Carrie's lawyer either to accept or reject. The lawyer accepted, according to what their letters say.

About this time, LaVere sent Sister Carrie a copy of the artwork that was to go with the Robert Johnson album. He wrote, "I think we should agree on a breakdown of the 16% royalty from the CBS release and attach it as a rider to our contract." He proposed that Carrie receive 4.4%. He added, "CBS is planning a Xmas release and we should see our first royalties by next June or July. They expect over

25,000 sets to be sold in the first 90 days and they will be wholesaling it at around $4.49! Count it up. It's something to look forward to."

Sister Carrie wasn't well, and I took a year off from my job to look after her. Lewis didn't exactly hobo, but he had gone down the road, and Charlyne's daughter had moved away, too, so Sister Carrie stayed on her own. We talked about Brother Robert and Steve LaVere, but mostly concentrated on surviving. It got to be my turn to look after Sister Carrie like she'd looked after Sister Bessie in her age.

Meanwhile, although we didn't know it at the time, LaVere had begun to get desperate. Mack McCormick was trying to block the release of the Robert Johnson record. He claimed that he owned the biographical material about Brother Robert that the album contained. He also said he'd found other heirs, a widow and children of Robert Johnson, knowing that they'd overtake Sister Carrie as sole heir. The record company didn't want to risk a lawsuit. On October 25, 1975, LaVere wrote to Sister Carrie's lawyer, "Let me tell you what's at stake here. John Hammond has put me in touch with one of, if not, the country's top copyright attorneys, who has advised me that all of Johnson's musical works are still copyright-able . . ."

The man LaVere dealt with at CBS Records was no fool—John Hammond. He'd tried to bring Brother Robert to New York in 1938 to play a concert after Brother Robert died.

The key part of LaVere's plan was to register himself as copyright holder of Robert Johnson's compositions. He continued explaining his plan to Sister Carrie's lawyer. "[I] have therefore rushed the formation of a publishing company to which CBS will give credit on their upcoming production. This means that over the next few years we should be able to collect on prior infringements, the sales of some of which number into the millions. At the standard rate of 2 [cents] per copy sold, you can see that if McCormick is successful in blocking the release of the new album, that he also will inhibit the collection of some hundreds of thousands of dollars, a 50% share of the net of which, of course, belongs to Carrie Thompson."

Without the record company giving credit to LaVere's publishing company as composer and publisher of Robert Johnson's music, LaVere couldn't collect the money that should have been coming in from musicians like Led Zeppelin and Eric Clapton who had recorded Brother Robert's songs.

The Robert Johnson record moved to the back burner, but LaVere kept working. He formed his King of Spades music publishing company and told Sister Carrie's lawyer about it in 1976, and said he'd retained a copyright attorney named William Krasilovsky.

Sister Carrie got a letter from a friend in North Carolina who helped her keep up with Lewis. The lady told Sister Carrie that Lewis planned to check in to "a A.A. home in Fayetteville, North Car. He told my son, as soon as he gets better, he is going to come out to see us. We will be glad to see him and hope he will soon be well again."

It wasn't to be. The next news that came to Sister Carrie was that Lewis had been found dead in a rooming house in Fayetteville. He was cremated and sent back to Maryland. He's buried in the cemetery with other members of our family.

CHAPTER 9

Steve LaVere's project of putting out the complete Robert Johnson record hit quite a few snags over the years. At one point, a man in New York named Robert Johnson came forward to claim the copyrights of Robert Johnson's music. He turned out to be a hoax. That Robert Johnson claimed he'd composed the songs, but admitted he didn't know Sister Carrie.

The biggest problem came from Mack McCormick. He didn't go away so easy. He stalled the release of the Robert Johnson record by threatening to sue.

June 9, 1977, LaVere wrote to Sister Carrie's lawyer, "As it now stands, CBS will release the album pending notification from Mack McCormick of his intentions. (They will send him a copy of the album liner notes and request that if he have any dispute, to notify them within 30 days.)"

Though Sister Carrie still worried that LaVere was a crook, he reported that he'd been taking care of business.

"I was also successful in obtaining affiliation with BMI on the songs. All the various infringements are being sorted out by BMI and myself now," LaVere wrote.

The release of the Robert Johnson record would have generated royalties from record sales and copyright infringements for Sister Carrie as Robert Johnson's undisputed heir.

Now all of a sudden, McCormick claimed to have a two-page contract with Sister Carrie—*after* he'd already brought up a flimsy typed-up document he'd thrown together when they met back in 1972. Sister Carrie didn't remember any two-page contract. McCormick had disappeared from her life after taking the photo of Brother Robert and Lewis and having her sign the authorization for him to write Brother Robert's biography. She kept the authorization form, and I still have her copy.

A letter attesting to Sister Carrie's contract with McCormick came to CBS Records from someone named Norris Stonecipher. He never explained who he was with regard to McCormick, and I know that LaVere doubted that Stonecipher even existed, he thought it was McCormick up to mischief. Whoever wrote the letter stated that McCormick "located several children, a widow, and other relatives who have primary claim to his estate. The heirs having reached an understanding among themselves are in process of petitioning a court of appropriate jurisdiction to appoint an executor for the estate of Robert Johnson. All concerned, having been traced by Mr. McCormick's monumental 8-year-long work, have entered into contracts as to biographical publishing rights and have been paid advance fees in good faith."

If any of this were true, these people would have taken precedence over Sister Carrie as Brother Robert's heir, but none of this ever happened. This threat delayed the release of the Robert Johnson record and halted any work being done on his biography due to legal questions about which of these white men rightfully owned Brother Robert's photographs and biographical information. Sister Carrie never got paid because of this. That's the reason I say I've dealt with some evil people.

Steve LaVere seemed to believe McCormick had found other heirs. He told Sister Carrie's lawyer, "I very much want to resolve this conflict with McCormick as it appears to be the only way to proceed. It's going to involve determining what rights he believes he has and making a decision at that point as to whether to refute his beliefs or be satisfied with what's left, which may be nothing, but then again, it might be the best piece of the pie: the copyrights and [music] publishing."

Around this time, Sister Carrie described a nightmare she'd had.

> [Two] white men [near] my house, they got out and went behind their truck, one twirled a rope and it went around a man's neck, [he] fell to the ground . . . the truck pulled up a little and backed over the man . . . I was in my drive way, saw it happened, tried to get the tag no . . . and ran back in the house thinking if he saw me that he might

come back and kill me . . . when I got in side, they was
a lot of hippys in here, and they were taking thangs out.
Robert was here . . . they had almost stripped the house
but it didn't look like my house inside, they was shelves
all around more like a store . . . these guys were putting
what they took out of the house in these cars. Funny, I
didn't seam mad, I said to Robert, "they took just about
every thang . . ."

"I was glad to wake up," she wrote.

The next subject in the letter was LaVere. "I wish I had never got into it at all . . . Just feel hopeless now, hate for the white man getting the benefit of what I should have, although according to God's word the unjust won't prosper."

With all this nonsense happening on Brother Robert's biography and record, Sister Carrie and I decided to take matters into our own hands. At that point, Sister Carrie turned over Brother Robert's few things to me.

"Anne I no you will do all you can to help with Robert's records and what ever can be got. I just don't know how to start," she wrote. "I feel that Lavere has something up his sleeve. I have no faith in him. I have no intention of letting him get me in his clutches again . . ."

She also gave me a great responsibility, to bring Brother Robert's legacy back to his family.

. . . it's up to you to use your own judgment, I am leaving
thangs up to you so do what you thank is best. I no this is

costing you money, all of these phone calls. My hands are tied, I have no money. I can't thank you enough . . . Now Bro Robert's death certificate is clear enough for you to read . . . also the paper of Robert's last words, which is very precious. He hadn't forgot his home training. Regardless of the life he lived wasn't near as bad as they are doing today. So I no that you will keep these papers, do what ever you thank best

You may not be able to understand this paper. I do. Will write it a little clearer:

Jesus of Nazareth, King of Jerusalem, Know that my Redeemer Liveth and that he will call me from the Grave

Thank of it

That's Strong words

From a dieing man

I don't spell to good either. Love, Sis Carrie

I went back to my teaching job in Boston after taking leave of absence to be with Sister Carrie. I paid lawyers fifty dollars here, fifty dollars there, none of them found anything. What we really wanted to do was open the Robert Johnson estate, none of them ever could. I could have copyrighted those photographs for Sister Carrie, if I'd had the right advice.

I never had gone into dives and wasn't really into blues, but I began to go to all the blues places around Boston. Lawyers never told me anything. I learned from the bluesmen. I learned that I was supposed to find where the assets were. To open an estate, the key was to find the money, any that Brother Robert's work was generating. I began learning a little about investigating. I started from nowhere.

Phoenix was the paper in Boston that advertised the blues shows. I saw an ad for Big Walter Horton and I decided to go and see if it's the Walter Horton I knew growing up in Memphis. I hadn't seen him since I went home to find him jamming with Brother Robert forty years before. I went to the Speakeasy in Cambridge, a very dark and crowded place. I'm walking through there looking at everybody for Walter Horton.

I hadn't seen him since I was ten years old, and I was looking for that young face I knew. I kept walking by him. Finally, a young man asked who I was looking for. That's where Professor Harp came in. He's a harmonica player who frequented the clubs. He ended up helping me a lot over the years. Professor Harp knew all the blues joints and he always saw me to my car. I never told him the business I was doing, but he helped make many introductions. First one, he pointed out Big Walter.

Walter had deteriorated. His jaw was sunken and his teeth had rotted. He remembered me well, because his sister went to school with me. He remembered how he used to call my sister "Auntie." He was just shocked to find someone who knew him from way back. I don't know of any harmonica player that topped Big Walter. He was melodious, he could be raucous. Of course they called him "Shakey" because of the way he blew. I thought they called him Shakey because he was an alcoholic, but it was about the vibration of the sound when he blew. I tell you, he was the boss harmonica player.

I asked him about how the business worked, but Big Walter was ignorant about his own money, he couldn't help much. He could barely write his name. He didn't get his money, they could beat him out of anything.

Here I was, over fifty years old, and on the nightlife for the first time. I talked to Willie Dixon, he tried to help me. Albert King, he didn't know Brother Robert but had heard of him. James Cotton, Sunnyland Slim, John Lee Hooker. I thought Brother Robert had to have come into contact with Howlin' Wolf, and asked Hubert Sumlin, Wolf's guitarist, but he came along after Brother Robert died. He just knew the name. Sunnyland also said he'd not been that close to Brother Robert, he's a pretty honest guy. Professor Harp introduced me to Muddy Waters. He said he knew of Brother Robert but hadn't known him.

I sat with Roosevelt Sykes throughout his breaks when he played the Speakeasy. He told me he used to take Brother Robert from Memphis to Hernando, Mississippi. He told me Brother Robert took "Sweet Home Chicago" from him, and I told him it was the other way around. He was very nice and I think he was honest. He said he'd throw Brother Robert's guitar in the trunk of his car.

I met Johnny Shines, a musician who'd told many stories about traveling and performing with Brother Robert. I know Johnny Shines embellished everything he said. I know Johnny Shines knew Robert Johnson, but not as well as he claimed. But if you want to get a little money, and tell white folks what they want to hear, they'll give you a few dimes. I can't dispute it, because I didn't have Brother Robert in my pocket. Brother Robert never talked about anyone he went around with. Johnny Shines, I don't see how he traveled to Chicago with Brother Robert, like he said he did, and didn't know about Uncle Will's barbershop on the South Side.

I had heard that Brother Robert sang a song called "Tell Me Mama," and I asked Johnny Shines about this. He looked at me strangely and said that was his song, and that he'd heard people in his family sing it.

Meanwhile, Steve LaVere was still scheming. He told Sister Carrie's lawyer, "Taking into consideration just the recordings [of Robert Johnson's songs] by the Steve Miller Band, Lynyrd Skynyrd, Eric Clapton, Fleetwood Mac, Johnny Winter, Youngbloods, Rolling Stones, Foghat, Taj Mahal, Paul Butterfield, Bonnie Raitt and Hot Tuna, there are 26 recordings that average at least a million sales or better each, which at the old statutory rate of 2 [cents] per copy, would have netted the publisher $520,000!"

He continued, "I hope that . . . gives you some idea of the magnitude of the possibilities in this matter." LaVere said a motion picture company was working on a movie about Robert Johnson, but told the lawyer, "I suggest that to avoid any disappointments, we refrain from informing Mrs. Thompson about any of this . . ."

CHAPTER 10

Sister Carrie got a new lawyer, Mr. Baldwin, based in Annapolis, Maryland. He initiated the process of rescinding her contract with Steve LaVere in early 1980. She wanted LaVere totally out of the picture when it came to collecting royalties on her behalf. Still, LaVere would have to agree to fully rescind the deal.

BMI is the music business clearinghouse that accrues royalty payments on copyrighted songs. Mr. Baldwin found out what LaVere had been up to with regards to collecting money from BMI.

In February 1976, LaVere and his attorney, Mr. Krasilovsky, got in touch with BMI. They presented BMI the contract between LaVere and Sister Carrie, outlining LaVere's ability to collect royalties for her. Krasilovsky had started King of Spades, LaVere's music publishing company, to collect money generated from Brother Robert's compositions. As I wrote to my sister at the time, "He was supposed to write a book on RLJ, not set up a publishing company!"

According to Mr. Baldwin, CBS Records had already recognized King of Spades' right to collect royalties by paying LaVere.

BMI wouldn't just give over to LaVere, though, he had to "clear" the songs, proving Brother Robert had composed them. This was difficult with Brother Robert's songs, because none of his written lyrics or music survived. To add to that, many blues songs were composed out of verses that many different musicians used, making it hard to establish an originator. A musicologist could also be hired to determine a song's authorship through research. After that, anybody who'd done one of Brother Robert's songs had to voluntarily pay, or else you'd have to take them to court.

BMI had started accruing royalties on Brother Robert's songs, though, and in early 1980 there was a "couple of thousand dollars," according to Mr. Baldwin. He spoke with a BMI lawyer who thought that LaVere had given up, faced with the challenges of clearing Brother Robert's songs. Mr. Baldwin let BMI know that Sister Carrie disputed LaVere's ability to collect royalties and BMI replied that it would hold all royalties until Sister Carrie and LaVere's dispute was settled.

Mr. Baldwin wrote,

> *It is my understanding that a rather modest sum was paid by CBS records to King of Spades Music, Inc. (formed by Stephen LaVere). In this regard, I note that*

Mr. LaVere apparently obtained a copyright as to Robert L. Johnson, although he has never divulged this information to his erstwhile principal Mrs. Thompson. The acknowledgment by CBS must have a certain degree of significance, even though BMI and other concerns feel there is an insufficient basis on which to acknowledge Carrie Thompson as the sole heir of Robert L. Johnson and hence entitled to accrued royalties.

So now we had to prove that Brother Robert's songs were Brother Robert's songs.

Rumors were going around the blues world that $100,000 had been collected for Brother Robert's next of kin. I saw Johnny Shines again with Robert Lockwood Jr. at Jonathan Swift's in Cambridge in October of 1980. They'd heard from a California lawyer who was looking for me to help get it.

Brother Robert had stayed with Lockwood's mother but hadn't married her, despite Lockwood sometimes calling Brother Robert his stepdaddy. Lockwood's wife was there, and she told me, "[Lockwood] is not entitled to any money, since his mother and [Robert Johnson] were not married, but he would be glad to help the family get the money. He would like to see it in their hands."

Lockwood had told me when I saw him at the Speakeasy two years before that he had a picture of Brother Robert, but now his wife asked me to send her one, so I didn't feel I could trust them. Muddy Waters had tried to get that photo from me of Brother Robert with the cigarette in his mouth. Johnny Shines spoke up and said he'd heard that Steve LaVere tried to sell a picture of Brother Robert for half a million dollars. He said, "that man has messed up everything he's ever touched. Don't sign anything."

I wanted to know if Lockwood had seen Brother Robert write any songs. They did mention some of the songs Brother Robert had composed, one in particular, "Steady Rollin' Man." That could be helpful.

Mr. Baldwin found a musicologist named Mr. Greenhill who offered to help our case. Sister Carrie wrote, "He said it would take lots of money to prove Robert Johnson's songs and music. He said all of the family and the ones who new him would have to get together. We would have to go to court."

Sister Carrie wrote to some people that she and Brother Robert had known.

In early 1981, Steve LaVere responded to Mr. Baldwin's notice that Sister Carrie wanted to rescind their contract. We hoped that we could prevent him from using our family photographs and the biographical information that Sister Carrie had provided during their interview back in 1974. "I feel that the Thompson/LaVere agreement should be renegotiated, but remain essentially intact. After all, it is through my efforts that Mrs. Thompson will be receiving monies and I feel I deserve a portion."

LaVere had some stationery made up with the letterhead "The Estate of Robert Johnson" and the photograph of Brother Robert wearing his pinstripe suit. LaVere had the photo marked with the copyright symbol next to his name, Stephen C. LaVere, and the year 1974.

This shocked Sister Carrie and me. We thought he'd lost his mind. No one had named LaVere as executor of the estate, the estate didn't exist. He hadn't formally copy-righted the photo, Sister Carrie had loaned it to him for use in his book. He just took these liberties. We lost any hope that he'd lost interest in the case and moved on.

LaVere had taken from my sister a photograph of our father, a photograph of her mother, and a photograph of Brother Son as well. Those weren't even addressed in the contract, and LaVere went and claimed to have copyrights on those photographs as well, when he had no business having those pictures.

Sister Carrie practically begged him to return all of her family photographs, including the copies of pictures he had of Brother Robert, but he claimed he needed the Brother Robert photographs, "to work with."

Sister Carrie had slowed down considerably. She still talked almost daily with Charlyne, and told me how she canned quarts of peaches and made her own wine. Her old house was hard to take care of, and she still had to mess with outdoor plumbing.

She signed over power of attorney to me in July 1981, but she kept writing letters to help clear Brother Robert's songs, and her lawyer told her she needed to prove she's Robert's sister. We wanted to establish that people had heard Brother Robert singing his songs, but old folks had a hard time remembering. She heard back from a friend in Robinsonville, Mississippi, who wrote her August 25, 1981. "I am 86 years old and can't think like I uster but my brother no you and your brothers, his name is Israel Clark and we all call him Wink—he come up with your brothers, Robert, he no he plaid the gitar . . . I hope you will have good luck, by from Lamon Mike Clark."

Mr. Clark was in the family of Doc Belton, the man who drove Brother Robert to Memphis from Mississippi for the Joe Louis fight.

Wherever we made contact, we found Steve LaVere had already been. One lady wrote Sister Carrie from Robinsinville, "Robert Johnson was just a very small boy, he always tried to make music, blowing bottles . . . yes, 2 or 3 white people be around asking about Robert . . . one of the men said you was going to get some money and he was going to send us one of Robert's records but we have not heard from him since."

Many people underestimated Sister Carrie. They thought she was just a sweet little old black lady. But she paid very close attention to what people said, and she studied their body language. When she met with one lawyer about the case, she saw how "he twitched his mouth with them plated teeth" and she could feel that he "wanted to move on to the money." She encouraged me to keep fighting for what we felt was ours. "What you are doing is brain work, and it is awful hard on the nerves." We worked with different lawyers, but ran into some attitude problems, as

Sister Carrie said of one, "He just couldn't take it, you being black and telling him off like you did."

Still, this work got to be too much on Sister Carrie. She wrote me, "I have worried over this almost ten years and these years of worrie has taken a toll." She was alone, since I was in Boston, and her grandson was in the army. My family had been divided up, too. My husband had a job in Barrington, Illinois, near Chicago.

With power of attorney, I began communicating with LaVere's attorney, Mr. Krasilovsky. We felt that Krasilovsky could have been more open about his pursuits of the Robert Johnson copyrights. He would never put anything in writing, he only wanted to talk by phone, and I refused to give out my number. I wanted to try and keep him on the record. As I told my sister, "Colonel Sanders didn't invent the Kentucky Fried Chicken recipe. He stole it from a black man. He told the truth on his deathbed. Whites never plan to deal fairly, so you have to be on your P's and Q's all of the time." So many lawyers had been so evasive, I got so I couldn't trust any of them anymore. They were always changing plans for what we needed to do, start a corporation, establish a trust. None of it mattered without the rights. We always struggled with the costs of all the attorneys and documents.

Sister Carrie lost considerable weight, and had trouble with her esophagus, which made eating unpleasant. She wrote to me, "This has been going on so long until I am worn out . . . and I hope you don't give out before we find out if there is any thang at the end of the Rainbow . . . I don't expect to live to reap all the benefits if there is any but I do want it to be in the family and not in the white mans pocket."

I stayed with her for the last months of her life. My daughter Sheila came down. My daughter and Sister Carrie had a good relationship.

Sister Carrie died February 20, 1983. I planned her funeral myself, and held the ceremony in Annapolis. It was well attended. I picked out three of her favorite songs and found a beautiful singer to perform. I remember best "Just a Closer Walk with Thee." She's laid to rest with our family members in Maryland. Her loss left me as our family's strongest link to Brother Robert, and the person who'd have to secure the estate of Robert Johnson.

CHAPTER 11

In 1986, *Rolling Stone* magazine published the photograph of Brother Robert with the cigarette hanging out of his mouth. LaVere listed himself as copyright holder. I think he waited until Sister Carrie was dead. At the time, I didn't know it happened. We still didn't have legal recognition as the legal heirs to the Robert Johnson estate.

That same year, the Rock & Roll Hall of Fame inducted Robert Johnson as an important early influence. I didn't hear from them and didn't know that had happened until much later.

In 1988, I moved to open the Robert Johnson estate. I went down to Greenwood, Mississippi, to meet with a lawyer. He wanted me to say I was Robert Johnson's niece. Well, that was a lie, to try and make me a blood relative. I consider myself the stepsister. I inherited my rights to Robert Johnson's music from Sister Carrie. In her will, she left Brother Robert's rights to me and her grandson,

Lewis's son Robert. People say I'm not Brother Robert's blood, but Steve LaVere had no more legal connection to Brother Robert than I did and far less personal connection. I brought her will to court as my power, and I'm still the administrator of her estate. I backed up my claim with birth certificates. We filed the petition to open the Robert Johnson estate. I had a hearing and gave a deposition. That took place in June of 1989, when I was named administratrix of the estate. I thought we'd finally got it done.

I stayed in touch with the blues scene around Boston. At one event, I saw this guy staring at me. He came over after about half an hour and introduced himself. It was John Hammond II. His father had tried to bring Brother Robert to New York back in 1938. The older John Hammond is the same man who'd been working with Steve LaVere to release Brother Robert's music on Columbia Records.

Hammond offered me a glass of wine. Normally, I don't accept drinks from anybody. He brought me a glass of Chablis. We sat down. He asked me, "Did you know Robert Johnson had a son?" I said, "There's no son." I told him if any son came in claiming, I'd file suit.

That was the first I heard of Claud Johnson. Mr. Hammond didn't use the name, though, he just used the term "son."

Mr. Hammond's father had died, but the *Complete Recordings of Robert Johnson* finally came out in August of 1990. Of course, it won a Grammy and sold a million copies. This was a shock. I had done my investigative research to find out where the assets were. I wrote Columbia and asked them about the masters of Brother Robert's recordings. I learned from reading about Prince and Dionne Warwick that you have to own your masters. Columbia said they didn't have it. I believed there weren't masters, but a short time later, my husband showed me an article in *USA Today* about that boxed set coming out, and how they had to have the masters to do it. Then I knew they had lied.

Steve LaVere wrote to me in October 1990, offering a share of 50 percent of the royalties *he* could earn for the estate. I never responded. If I got the estate, I wasn't about to split it with LaVere. I think he knew that. Sister Carrie's grandson and I considered ourselves the sole heirs of the estate of Robert Johnson.

Everything seemed to move very slowly in the Mississippi courts. In May of 1991, the Robert Johnson estate posted its notices to creditors and potential heirs. That's a routine public announcement that the estate's lawyer should have immediately taken care of, but it took him two years. Those notices brought some people out of the woodwork, relatives I had never heard of. There were some distant kin of Mama Julia's. And there came Claud Johnson. He claimed to be the illegitimate son of Robert Johnson.

Because of the *Complete Recordings*, the estate was worth some money. Steve LaVere got his without going to court—half the composer royalties for owning the copyrights. The other half went into an escrow account for the estate, but I never saw a penny.

As soon as Claud came forward, his lawyer had me removed from administering the estate. The chancery court in Greenwood, Mississippi, appointed its own clerk as administrator of the estate. The new administrator immediately signed a deal making Steve LaVere agent of the estate. Until then, the only legal support LaVere had was from the agreement he'd made with Sister Carrie in 1974, that she'd rescinded in 1980. The new contract gave LaVere power to "act for and on behalf of the Estate for the purpose of utilizing the name, likeness, and life story of Robert Johnson." The court-appointed administrator assigned ownership of Sister Carrie's property—those two photographs—to the estate. The deal with LaVere gave him legal control of those pictures.

My lawyer moved to have Claud's claim dismissed. The judge dismissed Claud's claim as being time barred. But Claud appealed, saying that I hadn't performed my administrative duties and had deprived him of his rights as potential heir by not attempting to locate him. Really it was my Mississippi lawyer. He let two years go by from when I opened the estate until he posted the notice to heirs.

I saw Claud's marriage certificate from 1952. The document lists his father as "R. L. Johnson," with an address of New Orleans, Louisiana. It didn't say Robert Johnson, and it didn't say he was deceased. Even if Claud thought he was alive, Brother Robert never lived in New Orleans. On Claud's birth certificate, the father is listed as "R. L. Johnson" from Memphis, but Johnson's age is listed as "don't know."

Later, it came out that I couldn't have found Claud Johnson anyway—for most of his adult life he went by the last name of his stepfather, Cain.

By 1995, it was known that LaVere had paid over $800,000 into the estate.

We came back to court in 1998. For the first time, I looked Claud Johnson over. He's short and stumpy. He didn't have the slender face, the long fingers. I didn't see any resemblance.

In court, Claud's lawyers played a videotaped interview of Claud's mother, Virgie Jane Smith Cain. She had died recently. She said she had met Brother Robert when she was seventeen years old. She saw him playing guitar at a supper and later met him at her aunt's house. She said she remembered Brother Robert playing "Terraplane Blues," even though that automobile came out in 1932. She said she'd never had sex with anyone before Brother Robert, and didn't with anyone else until she married, three years after meeting Brother Robert. She claimed that the first time she was with Brother Robert had happened while she was walking to school, in September of 1931. She delivered Claud in December of that year. How that's possible, I don't know. She said that she and Brother Robert were together two more times, both at her aunt's house while her aunt was out. When a lawyer asked if there'd been any other times with Brother Robert, she said, "It might have been. You know, that's been a long time ago, and I don't remember things anymore."

The bomb came from Mrs. Cain's friend, Eula Mae Williams. She also did not appear in court. Her testimony came from an older videotaped recording, like Mrs. Cain's. Mrs. Williams said she had seen Brother Robert and Mrs. Cain having sex in the woods on a cold night. That struck me as different from what Mrs. Cain had said about being with Brother Robert on her way to school, not at night, and in her aunt's house, not in the woods.

Mrs. Williams said that she and her husband were out there with Brother Robert and Mrs. Cain. "We were all doing the same thing."

But Mrs. Cain said she and Brother Robert were alone in the woods and only told Mrs. Williams about that later on. Mrs. Williams said she saw them together in the woods three times before Mrs. Cain said she'd gotten pregnant. So, the stories didn't really add up.

When court went into recess, the judge went over to Claud Johnson and laughed and joked. I turned to my lawyer and said, "You can forget it, this case is gone." The judge should have never been over there. They didn't want that money getting out of Mississippi.

My family lost all we worked for during the past twenty-five years because a woman said that she saw Brother Robert making love to her friend, over fifty years before. You know, I was born at night, but not last night.

I don't know when I conceived, who does? That's when it hit me. How did some other woman know when Claud's mother conceived? That sounds like a lie. This woman couldn't know if Claud's mother had been with someone else, or what Claud's mother's schedule was. But it went through, and the courts ruled on it. They announced in court that Claud Johnson was Robert Johnson's sole heir. I felt dumbfounded. I couldn't believe it. I had never heard of this guy. I said so. I am tough, and I can lose my temper and get a little mouthy.

The judge even said there was doubt about the strength of Claud's evidence, and he shared his opinion that splitting the estate between our group and Claud would be the fairest result. The judge relied upon Claud's birth certificate, listing R. L. Johnson as the father. My lawyer showed that a birth certificate of an illegitimate child that lists a father without the father's input was illegal as of 1931, Claud's birth year. According to Mississippi paternity law, an illegitimate child had to provide clear and convincing evidence to establish his father in a case like this one. That information came from Claud's mother who said, at the time of Claud's birth, that this R. L. was a laborer residing in Memphis. She knew him as a musician who lived near her in Copiah County, Mississippi.

Claud waited until he was the age of sixty-one to come forward and claim to be Brother Robert's son. For most of his life, he'd gone by his mother's husband's last name. When Claud applied for a new social security card in 1992—after he'd put in his claim as Robert Johnson's son—he stated that his father was Pluchie Cain, the man his mother had married.

I wish I could come out and say exactly what happened. Everyone would deny it and try to sue. I wish someone could come in and dissect the whole case. Not having any money, I wasn't in a position to fight. I didn't have the right lawyer. The lawyer tried to push the theory that Brother Robert could not have conceived. The back of Brother Robert's death certificate states that syphilis might have been a cause of death. The lawyer said that could have made Brother Robert sterile. He didn't get into the mistakes and errors in the testimony about Brother Robert conceiving Claud. They refused to do DNA testing. I understand that Claud has gone on, but his son is still alive. If it's true that Robert Johnson fathered Claud, then Claud's son and Sister Carrie's grandson Robert, who's still alive, are both Mama Julia's great-grandsons. There was talk of exhuming Mama Julia's body, but she can't be found because of the flood waters.

No court made Steve LaVere pay Sister Carrie for the use of her property, those two well-known photographs, that Sister Carrie kept safe for forty years, and for the biographical information she supplied for the booklet that went with the *Complete Recordings*. Everyone who's ever written about Brother Robert owes her. All of the information about our family that they use came from Sister Carrie. Our fight wasn't only about the royalties. Claud Johnson didn't give LaVere photographs or biographical information. He didn't know anything. We treasured

Brother Robert and his memory all those years when it wasn't worth any money, just out of our love for him.

LaVere was a crook from his heart. Sister Carrie was taken under.

We appealed the decision and lost, in 2000.

CHAPTER 12

I traveled to Mississippi in September of 2001. A man named Paul Cartwright invited me to come to Hazlehurst, the town my father had been run off from, where Brother Robert was born. Mr. Cartwright came to pick me up in Jackson, and he took me to Hazlehurst. He's a librarian and he'd done so much research on my family. He found the house my father built.

I got to see the home for the first time. Just to see my father's work was amazing. I knew he was a carpenter, but the Doric columns he put on that house shocked me. I was in pain with my knee, but I managed to get up on that porch and peep inside the house. I was afraid to go in because it's all propped up. I appreciate Mr. Cartwright doing a lot of work on that house. He moved it to a better location. It still needs restoration.

I went through town and the saw the train station, where my father had escaped.

The mayor wanted to see me. I couldn't imagine why a mayor wanted to see me.

This guy came up and talked to me. He introduced himself and wanted to ask for forgiveness for the way the Marchetti man had attacked my father and driven my father away from home and family. I was stunned. I couldn't even move. I can still see him walking away. I was left standing in my tracks. I never answered him. There was nothing to forgive him for, he wasn't even thought of. I wish I could see him again to tell him. There's nothing to forgive. I would like for that to take place, because I would never blame someone for what their parents did.

In the 50s I went back to Memphis, so my girls could visit their grandmother. I went to visit friends at 695 Short Hernando. The Comases had moved to California. My sister Charlyne was still in Memphis. She said the Comases came back to visit and little Betty could gamble like a man. Of course, her father was a gambler. In the '50s the neighborhood hadn't changed.

I went to Memphis again in 1982. I drove down to get my sister. We stayed at the Peabody, just a short distance from our home on Georgia Avenue. I went to look at the old place. A family lived there. The shed my father had built for Patsy was upright and the hedges were where I remembered them, the path through the garden to the bayou could still be seen.

Now most of the homes in the neighborhood have been torn down. On the eightieth anniversary of Brother Robert's death, I sat at the edge of the bayou out front of

Mrs. Annye C. Anderson, August 16, 2018, at site of Robert Johnson's family home. Memphis. *Photo by Preston Lauterbach*

our old house. It's falling in and abandoned, except for where a homeless person had a pallet.

Over the years, I saw the books, magazine features, and documentary films about Brother Robert come and go, and I never wanted to participate. Some of them lean on the sexual stuff, and I've had to tell them, "Get a life." The stories about his dealing with the devil took away from his real talent. I thought if that's how it's going to be, they can't have him. I always turned down interview requests, because I didn't want to be mixed up with lies. Plus, I always remembered that Brother Robert got peanuts for his recordings. I said I'd never get caught in that.

I felt that I had to protect the real Brother Robert that I knew. He didn't get his abilities from God or the Devil. He made himself. People have stuck Brother Robert's family off to the side, because it makes him more interesting to be a vagabond or a phantom. And it makes him easier for someone else to make money off of if we're out of the picture.

But I know now, at my age, once I go, the real Brother Robert goes, forever. I don't want the myths and lies to surround him. I had to wait until now to tell my own story my own way.

I don't believe he's buried behind a church, and they've claimed he's buried behind three different churches. There should be a law against taking people's money on these bus tours that show them these gravesites. Black people are serious about religion. That's what held us back, we're too religious. We believed we'd be taken into Heaven, instead of collecting something down here, like whites. We're into that. I've heard a Baptist preacher say, "Do as I say and not as I do," but I don't believe that a minister would have allowed a sinner to be buried in their churchyard. I think he's in a potter's field, as I have been told. There is no grave marker, because we could not afford one.

I am proud that he's been recognized by the Rock & Roll Hall of Fame, and with a Grammy, and that so many great artists have said nice things about him. In a way I took him for granted. I didn't see him that important. It's hard even now to think that he was this great. I just knew him as Brother Robert. I have to give the British boys a lot of credit for building that, for popularizing Robert Johnson. Mama Julia used to say she made one mistake, having Robert out of wedlock, but that the Lord forgave her. If she could come back today, she'd see it was no mistake.

I understand that Steve LaVere has gone on, and Mack McCormick, too. But there are others and always will be: white men who don't know us and think they own us. Steve LaVere may be resting in a golden casket that Brother Robert bought him.

I have only one story left to tell, and one more glimpse to show of the real Robert Johnson.

There was a make-your-own-photo place on Beale Street, near Hernando Street. I've since learned that a man named John Henry Evans owned it. The photo place was right next door to Pee Wee's, the bar where Mr. Handy wrote his blues. One day when I was ten or eleven years old, I walked there with Sister Carrie and Brother Robert. I remember him carrying his guitar and strumming as we went. You just walk in, drop a nickel in the slot, pull the curtain and do it. There was no photographer. I had my picture made. Brother Robert got in the booth, and evidently made a couple.

I kept Brother Robert's photograph in my father's trunk that sat in the hallway of the Comas house while we lived there with my mother after my father died. After my mother died, we could only take so many things. I took my photographs with me, wrapped in a handkerchief. I only carried a few belongings to Ma and Pops Thompson's house. When I moved in with my sister Charlyne,

I bought some furniture. I stored the photograph, along with others, in a cedar chest I bought. I've always had this photograph.

It shows Brother Robert the way I remember him— open, kind, and generous. He doesn't look like the man of all the legends, the man described as a drunkard and a fighter by people who didn't really know him. This is my Brother Robert.

AN INTERVIEW WITH
MRS. ANNYE C. ANDERSON

Peter Guralnick (PG), Elijah Wald (EW), and Preston
Lauterbach (PL) Interview Mrs. Annye C. Anderson (AA)

Elijah Wald, Mrs. Annye C. Anderson, and Peter Guralnick, May 2, 2019,
Massachusetts. *Photo by Preston Lauterbach*

May 2, 2019, Amherst, Massachusetts

PG: I love how you talk about Robert Johnson entertaining the kids.

AA: He loved children, and he'd sit in the window picking his guitar, and we'd come up. The grown folks were doing the cakewalk, and we did the snakehip. Those old dances, we weren't into that.

PG: What was the Joe Louis dance?

AA: Joe Louis was trucking. That's what I did when I slipped off to the Amateur Night at the Palace. I remember the "One O'Clock Jump" was the music that you came on with. I went out and I got a couple of boos, but mostly I didn't.

PL: Who would boo you?

AA: My neighbor, Jimmy Crawford, he was a young boy who lived in our neighborhood, on Short Hernando.

Sister Carrie had made me a three-tiered dress, with white cap sleeves. And I had learned to iron, I had ironed that dress. Somebody had given me some patent leather slippers and I had those little socks on that the Chinese made—you don't see those now, but they had beautiful stuff from China.

Back then, children either wanted to be a movie star or they wanted to sing. But as you grow up, you find there are other areas: I wanted to be a nurse at one time, a doctor at one time, and then a teacher.

EW: Did you know [Robert's stepfather] Mr. Willis?

AA: We all did. We were family, and knew him well. We'd visit them. They always came to our house. Mister Willis, I know he was a workaholic, he loved working. In the fields, because that's all he knew. He had an impediment of speech. Growing up, we called it tied-tongue. If he wanted to say the word "girl" it came out "dirl."

There was no animosity between Mama Julia, Mister Willis, and my mother and father. I read in a book about Mister Willis and Brother Robert not getting along. Because I was young, I never saw it. My father is depicted as an unkind man, but my father was very laid back. He never punished us, he didn't believe in whipping children. Sister Carrie said he never touched her. Sister Carrie was a very good child, according to Mama Julia. I can't say that for me. I got some spankings from my mother, but my father didn't believe in that.

Mama Julia was smart—busy, busy, busy—and a *little* woman. When I was seven years old, I could look across her head. We used to save newspaper and send it down to Mama Julia and Sister Bessie, down in Mississippi. Their walls were all covered with newspaper.

EW: To keep the wind from coming in?

AA: That, and also to keep the raw wood from showing. They used it as if it were paint.

EW: Did they use pages with pictures, so it would look nice?

AA: No. It was just the *Press-Scimitar* and the *Commercial Appeal*, that's what we took.

PG: How about the *Memphis World*?

155

AA: We took that—all of those black papers, like *Chicago Defender*.

PG: Was everybody a reader?

AA: My father read every day, and he only had a seventh grade education—but he took the paper. My mother only had a fifth grade education, but she read what she could. My father had a very legible hand. I had letters from Mama Julia, my sister Bessie. I still have writings from my Sister Carrie, she was the better educated one of all.

EW: Robert could read and write?

AA: Could read and write. He read the paper, because if you look at Ethiopia—that's when Haile Selassie was all popular, all blacks wanted to know about him—and he uses the term Ethiopia [in "Dust My Broom"], there's a connection with that.

EW: But the songs, did he ever write them down?

AA: People talk about him carrying a little book, but I can't imagine him carrying, it was enough for him to carry the pickers that he had. I've never seen and Sister Carrie said she's never seen a book, and he lived with her off and on. At 728 Hernando, they only had three rooms, the bedroom, a living room, and a kitchen. All the rooms were good-sized but not overly big. He always slept in the bedroom.

EW: When you talk about his picks . . . did he make those himself or were they store-bought?

AA: I guess some of them were store-bought. I have

known him to use a thimble. I have known him to use a beef bone.

EW: What would he use thimbles for?

AA: Slides. If he couldn't find the real one. As a makeshift.

EW: It would be very fine, on one string, but he did that kind of playing, it makes sense.

PG: Did Robert go to school in Memphis?

AA: I don't know which school. I know he went to at least the eighth grade, by his age when he left my father. He was a teenager when he left my father.

PG: Some say he went to school in Commerce [Mississippi] after that.

AA: He did, briefly, but he was a big boy by then. And I'm pretty sure he wasn't there long. He was fourteen when he left my father. Then he went to his mother's house. At seventeen he married, and went to my Brother Granville and Sister Bessie's. By the way, he was around two ministers. So the devil and hellfire and crossroads, I'm pretty sure arose from their sermons. He was flanked by two ministers and a very religious mother. Mama Julia was very religious.

PG: You never knew him to go to church though?

AA: No, Mama Julia and Sister Bessie were the churchgoers.

EW: Did Brother Robert make up songs all the time?

AA: I never saw him make up any song, I never saw him write a song, I don't think any of us saw him write anything, and I've never seen a notebook. What I have seen is all his paraphernalia that he laid out on the table. I know his repertoire pretty well. He was blues, he was folk, he was country. Jimmie Rodgers was his favorite, and he became my favorite. Brother Robert could yodel just like he did. We did "Waiting for a Train," together.

EW: You talk about the different kinds of places where he played, did he play the same repertoire every place?

AA: He and Son played together a lot, that's his brother [Charles Leroy].

People liked "Sweet Home Chicago" and "Kind Hearted Woman," and, of course, "Terraplane." "Take a Little Walk with Me" would be the break-up time. You know . . . that's it. You're gonna break up. That's the end of the entertainment. The children liked the ones you could up tempo, like "Last Fair Deal." He could do that for us, and we could do all the twisting we wanted to do. Nursery rhymes, when we were little, "Jack and Jill," "Little Sally Walker," "We Go Lokey, Lokey, Lokey," have you heard that one?

EW: No.

AA: [singing] We go lokey, lokey, lokey on this bright and summer day; you put your right foot in, you take your right foot out; you take your something and you shake your body around . . .

And you name it. All the Irish songs he did, because in the South they used to sing lots of those songs: "Annie Laurie," "My Bonnie," and "Auld Lang Syne."

Jimmie Rodgers was going to come up in all his entertainment, because I could sing that along with him.

PG: Could you yodel?

AA: No, I couldn't yodel, but I know how it goes, and when he comes in, I know "All around the water tank, waiting for a train . . ." Brother Robert would do a double-take on "get off, get off, you railroad bum."

EW: You mention Brother Robert showing you something on piano at one time.

AA: No, playing with Son.

EW: So Robert didn't play piano?

AA: Yes, he did. I don't know how much he knew, but the boogie-woogie, he and Son used to play together. Brother Robert hit the heavy notes, the black notes, and my brother Son, he hit the ivory keys. He was a pianist.

EW: So the two of them played on one piano?

AA: On one piano. That was at the Comases on Short Hernando. They had a long hallway, and that piano belonged to Miss Willie. They had the player piano, with the rolls on it, and that's where they entertained.

PL: Do you remember any songs they played on the piano?

AA: As a child, I liked the boogie-woogie, but they played Leroy Carr. That was Son. He played all of the Leroy Carr songs, "When the Sun Goes Down," "How Long How Long Blues," I remember that one. And there's another one, another pianist, Fats Waller—we all loved Fats Waller. Son would do Fats Waller, he would clown.

And Louis Armstrong was a household word. Brother Son would play the piano, and Brother Robert would just pick up anything and get the tune on it.

PG: When Brother Robert sang his own songs, did he introduce them, say "Here's a new song," how would you know, did he differentiate between his songs?

AA: He didn't, and I had no idea, it would never occur to me whether he created them or not. I just knew "Kind Hearted Woman" and "Terraplane" was his, he let us know about the record. We got it at Woolworth's down on Main Street. My sister Charlyne used to decorate the window there. How I knew he recorded all those songs, was when I came to Amherst, I met a young man named Ed Cohen. He worked for WMUA, a radio station at the University of Massachusetts. He told me, "I'm going to play all twenty-nine." I stayed up late that night and listened to every one. I was completely shocked.

EW: When you heard those recordings, were some of them new or were you familiar with all of them?

AA: I had heard all of them.

PG: Even something like "Hellhound on My Trail"?

AA: Oh yeah, well there's a history on that hellhound. You'll find many black people who talk about the hellhound. The connection is the white overseer. I've heard my sister Bessie say she went in the field and saw a hound. The hound is always white. He's heard it and put that in his music.

PG: So, hellhound could refer to the bible, but it could also go back to slavery times.

AA: Right, I know when people talk about the hellhound, they see it in the field.

He might not have gone past the eighth grade, but he was very intelligent. He did read the paper, he did know some history. He and Son used to joke about, in slavery, you didn't cook in the big house, you cooked in an out building and brought the food in. They sent a dog along with the slave to make sure they don't eat any of it. A lot of tales I've heard them talk about.

PG: Would everyone be aware of Marcus Garvey? Joe Louis was a race hero . . .

AA: Well, honey . . . Two things he was into, and that was the baseball, the Negro League, and Joe Louis. Everybody was into Joe Louis.

PG: Was he a fan of the Memphis Red Sox, Negro League team?

AA: I don't know whether he was into that or not, I know he went to see the live ones play in Arkansas.

EW: You talk about Robert enjoying Western movies, did you listen on the radio to stuff like that?

AA: Oh yeah, Bulldog Drummond, the Lone Ranger—I don't know if the Lone Ranger was on when *he* was living, I don't think so. The ball games, Brother Robert, Ma, and Sister Carrie, they listen to all of it. I don't know whether he listened to soaps, but I know the women did, cause that meant I could leave and go anywhere, and come back just in time.

PG: Gene Autry?

AA: That was a household word. Son did "That Silver-Haired Daddy of Mine"—sometimes they played it together.

EW: Did Robert have favorite movie actors?

AA: Yeah, Buck Jones. He was a tough guy. He became my favorite. Gene Autry could sing, so we all loved him.

EW: Were there other kinds of movies he liked?

AA: At that time most of what you saw were Westerns, but he went to see Mae West, Errol Flynn.

PG: Did you see people like Mantan Moreland?

AA: Oh, yes, I'm familiar with Mantan Moreland, with the Bronze Buckaroo. We loved Mantan Moreland.

PG: Paul Robeson is somebody that Robert would have been aware of?

AA: Yes, Paul Robeson was a household word. He was very aware of what was going on around him—the wars, the news, Ethiopia, Haile Selassie . . . Brother Robert was into his blackness. He knew he was black. When he tells you he doesn't want sundown to catch him here, he knew exactly what had gone on.

PL: When you talk about Irish music being popular in Memphis, does that come out of what you were taught in school?

AA: Yeah, that's what I learned. [Robert] would play with me if I sang "Auld Lang Syne." We always sung the Negro National Anthem, we were allowed to do that.

EW: You mentioned Big Walter Horton, did he play with Robert?

AA: Yes he did, they played "Little Boy Blue," "Sittin' on Top of the World." I sat with his sister Katie in school.

EW: Did Robert ever play with horn players?

AA: I don't remember him hooking up with a horn. The only group I saw him with was at the Comases, with Memphis Minnie, and there were some other people, but I don't remember any horns. But those were adult entertainers, we were on the porch, eating watermelon.

A man would come through selling watermelons, you can get a huge watermelon for a dime. And I don't want to forget that red hot—Brother Robert's talking about the hot tamale man, the Mexicans used to come through and sing and have those, and they were the best-tasting hot tamales. And the watermelon man would come around late at night. "I got one for nickel, two for a dime, would give you more but they ain't none of mine." You know, he may have picked up [on] some of that, but certainly the hot tamales and they are red hot.

EW: Speaking about food, how about the song he did, "Malted Milk"?

AA: That malted milk was in the house. Now, whether liquor was in it . . . See, I was young, and back then two things didn't happen: you didn't drink around your parents, and you respected your mother.

PG: Your father's friends from Hazlehurst, the Comases, who were your neighbors in Memphis, would have parties . . .

AA: In the hallway, it was a huge hallway that ran the length of the house, I think they refer to that as a shotgun house.

PG: People would know there was a party at the Comases . . .

AA: Everybody could come. The lady across the street would come, because there would be noise. "If it gets too noisy, come on over."

PG: It wasn't a rent party . . .

AA: Oh they had rent parties, funerals, and Brother Robert played at some fish fries and barbecues. My uncle Cross could fry chicken and fish, buffalo fish that come out of the Mississippi River, huge fish. We used to get carp, perch, trout, eel. Yeah, used to fish in the Mississippi River, that's one of the sports I love.

EW: Did Robert go fishing?

AA: He went one time, with Mr. Martzie. We had to walk down, over the bluff and to the Mississippi River. Brother Robert thought he would fish, he tied the line around his toe. We did a throw line, we made ours out of bamboo. Sister Bessie taught me how to make a "throw line." She taught me how to bait and how to fish, and when I visited her, that's where we went. We fished in the bar pit—that's where the water's made to come in between the levee, when the Mississippi overflows, and in between you call that a bar pit. That was in Robinsonville, Mississippi. But this was in Memphis: Brother Robert tied the line on, and an eel got on it, and that's a fighting fish, honey. That eel got on and almost broke that toe off. That was very funny to us. He went hopping across the Harahan Bridge into Arkansas.

EW: When Robert came back from his travels, would he ever tell you stories about where he had been?

AA: I don't know whether he told any of us where he'd been, but I know he and Son hoboed together. I've seen them catch the train, at the switch, when the train slows down. Son came back when they went to Mexico with a few Mexican words. Only one I picked up was señorita. Son used to talk about the pretty girls there. Son traveled by train by himself, too. They didn't always go together, but they did go everywhere. My mother had a first cousin in California, Alonzo. I never knew his full name. I told that to

Johnny Shines, and the next thing I knew, he'd given my words to a writer who published the exact ones in his book! People pick up anything and to be honest, they'll tell white folks anything for a dime.

PL: Did you grow up thinking Robert was your full-blood brother?

AA: Yes. We were family, and everything was fine until he recorded and people begin to get jealous. When he recorded, you had people saying, "That's not your brother." Every time I said, "Brother Robert," somebody said, "That's not your brother." Well I was taught to call him and that's all I've ever called him, so it comes naturally.

PL: He did have a different last name, were you always aware of that?

AA: No, no. I knew him as a brother, and he was always a brother. I was Baby Sis or Little Sis. Have you seen my poem I've written? When I was a little girl, small enough to set upon his knee. He used to play his many many tunes, just for me. Nobody believed that Brother Robert had any kin people, they felt that he was a vagabond.

EW: Did any of the women in the family play music?

AA: There's some kind of music line that runs through the family. Sister Bessie played organ and piano. In the house my father built in Hazlehurst, they had two parlors, and there was an organ there. My father talked to me about that house. The pump was in the kitchen—that was really something back then.

EW: Did Robert play any other instruments?

AA: He was playing harmonica when he came and got us from Eudora, Mississippi, when I was three years old. He was living with Sister Bessie. We had to move at night. Most blacks did, Mama Julia has had to move at night. Yeah, hellhound on her trail.

EW: When Robert played harmonica, did he play things like "Fox Chase"?

AA: You know what, I had to connect it [later], because I didn't know anything about the "Fox Chase" but I knew he played the harmonica, because he'd give the harmonica to Lewis, and from Lewis, we'd get it. It came from Brother Robert, to Lewis, to us. Lewis never learned to blow it, and we never learned to blow it, but Brother Robert could blow it. But we did not call it harmonica, that was not in our vocabulary. We called it "juice harp"—and not Jew's—we called it juice because when you blew, you get the juice in it.

PG: You talked at one point about how Robert wanted to be a modern blues man, he didn't want to be old-fashioned.

AA: Well, that's what I wanted to portray. He was contemporary at that time. A lot of people didn't like him. My neighbor liked Sonny Boy and Broonzy, before Brother Robert. Because he was different. He was definitely different.

EW: What was different about him?

AA: There was no slide going the way he played the slide. And I've heard them all.

PG: If Robert had lived, where do you think he would have gone with his music? Jazz for instance?

AA: He played jazz with Son. I hate to say rock 'n' roll, but . . . people move on from classical blues music, Brother Robert would have moved on. He may have been playing something completely different. He was versatile, he played jazz, along with his brother.

He and Son went everywhere. That's why I say I didn't have him in my pocket. I can't relate to him getting drunk and cursing God. I've never seen him take a drink, but I can't say he did not drink, cause the liquor was there. Old Grand-Dad, that's what my father drank. When we had house parties, there would be a coal box filled with ice and beer. Beer was served. But I've never seen him drunk or drink alcohol. And I can't say that he didn't, but I can't imagine him picking a fight. I remember him as asking all the guests, and even the children, "What's your pleasure?" That is him saying, "What do you want to hear?"

PL: Did you ever know Brother Robert to play with white musicians?

AA: No, I never knew, but I know he hung around rodeos. He loved Texas. He and Jimmie Rodgers had a lot in common, Texas, TB, trains. I know he went to Mexico, California, he went everywhere out west.

PL: In your youth, when you listened to country music, did you feel like there was common ground with blues music?

AA: What I get most out of country music, I know it comes out of Irish music, and I can hear it. I know that country music is a combination of Irish music and blues. History tells me that country music came out of blues.

PG: What about Robert playing that boogie-woogie figure on guitar?

AA: You talking about the walking bass?

PG: Yeah, walking bass, did he always do that?

AA: Yeah, that's his. I never heard any other musician play that until after Robert Johnson had done it. I feel that he invented it.

PG: That would be one way he was modern.

AA: I call it contemporary.

EW: As far as anybody knows, that was original to Robert Johnson.

PG: But you said Robert would play the bass end of the piano with Son.

AA: He played the heavy bass, of course, honey, we loved that. The piano was out of tune, but they'd make it work.

EW: Do you think Robert Johnson started playing it that way on guitar, because he was copying what he could do on piano?

AA: That I couldn't say.

Afterword:
Brother Robert's Beale Street

By Preston Lauterbach

During **Brother Robert's** time, people called Beale "the Main Street of Black America." Much more than a hangout for blues musicians, Beale had a storied history, a cast of colorful current characters, and a list of lively venues, from low-down dives to first-class theaters infusing the atmosphere around Johnson.

In February of 1937, Dan Burley of the *Chicago Defender* visited Beale and reported, "The street has everything dumped into it: proud insurance companies, stinky hotdog joints, swank hotels, and myriad poolrooms, push carts, peanut vendors, drugstores, shoeshine parlors, and automobiles." Still, the street had more spirit than space. This activity filled all of five or six blocks from the Mississippi River to the eastern residential end of Beale.

The street had gained its fame due to two individuals, Robert Church and W. C. Handy, known, respectively, as the South's first black millionaire and the father of the blues. The world that Robert Church made, that had inspired W. C. Handy, still existed in Brother Robert's time, though Church had died in 1912 and Handy had left Beale Street for Broadway in 1918.

Church, born into slavery in 1839, made his fortune owning saloons, gambling halls, brothels, and residential real estate. He nurtured talented African Americans like journalist Ida B. Wells, and Handy, the composer who wrote songs based on the sounds he heard in Beale saloons, and helped start the blues craze.

Beale Street historian George W. Lee said, of the heyday, "Nightly Beale Street was crowded. People would move down the street like molasses poured out of a jar and nightly you could hardly worm your way through Beale Street, packed and jammed and jangling and colorful and roaring and glamorous."

Beale Street's beginnings as a black music hub probably date to the antebellum days, when urban slaves on shopping errands heard fiddler Wesley Duke (known also as West Dukes) at the Beale Street market house.

Robert Johnson's top Beale Street venue seems to have been the open air Handy Park, a grassy square with benches and a few trees where the market house once stood. Visiting the park in 1937, *Defender* correspondent Burley heard a "group of farm boys with banjos and spoons beatin' out melody that'd make Duke Ellington forget his 'When a Black Man's Blue.'"

Memphis blues recording artists like Bukka White played Handy Park, along with guitarists Jack Kelly and Frank Stokes, banjo player Gus Cannon, and ukulele player Little Laura Dukes. Sleepy John Estes, a blues artist from Brownsville, Tennessee, got to Beale Street in about 1928, and met musicians Jim Jackson, Buddy Doyle, Will Batts, and several other jug band performers.

Hammie Nixon, a jug blower from Brownsville who recorded in the 1920s and played Handy Park said, "Beale Street was full of conning . . . I knew a girl there who would just put her hand around your neck and say 'Hey baby,' and she had you and every dime you had."

Robert Johnson's friend Walter Horton, another regular at Handy Park, grew up on Third Street near Beale. Walter sold ice on the Beale Street fish dock on the Mississippi River for his first job, and he shined shoes beside Solvent Savings Bank, founded by Robert Church as the city's first African American financial institution. Walter's mother worked for the Barrasso family—owners of the Palace and Daisy theaters. Walter helped build the New Daisy, and he ushered and played Amateur Night at the Palace. He grew up attending First Baptist Church, Beale Avenue, one of the few historic buildings still fully intact, where he learned to play gospel music.

Mrs. Anderson remembers jug bands parading through her neighborhood en route to Beale. The March 19, 1938 *Chicago Defender* reported that the South Memphis Jug Band was headquartered on Cambridge Street,

about a mile and a half from the Spencer home. The South
Memphis Jug Band lineup, led by a hoodoo doctor named
D. M. Higgins, included Will Batts and Jack Kelly. Batts
had made records under his name and with the jug band
in 1933. In 1937, Batts lived less than a mile from 285 E.
Georgia Avenue.

These Beale Street musicians who were overlooked in
the '30s made a far greater impact on history than the popular local musicians of the same period. Memphis musicians named in the *Defender* during summer 1938 are now
virtual unknowns, including Andrew Chapman, a local
drummer who'd caught the eye of Duke Ellington, saxophonist Hank O'Day, and Dub Jenkins, leader of a popular
local big band out of the Orange Mound neighborhood.
The Brown Skin Models entertained at the Palace and an
all-girl jazz big band known as the International Sweet-
hearts of Rhythm were hired to play the Cottonmakers Ju-
bilee, an annual Beale Street festival.

Big-time acts like Fats Waller—"Son" Spencer's
favorite—and Jimmie Lunceford did sold-out shows on
Beale Street in 1938. One radio program reliably broad-
cast black music in Memphis during summer 1938, the
fifteen-minute "Rhythm Club" weekday afternoons at two
on WHBQ. The show typically featured recordings of a
name bandleader like Lunceford or Chick Webb.

Mrs. Anderson recalls how Robert and his brother
"Son" enjoyed listening to Clyde McCoy, a white trumpeter
and bandleader who'd had a hit with "Sugar Blues." Mc-
Coy played trumpet with a mute, blotting and roughing-up

his notes, a sound that helped inspire development of the Vox Clyde McCoy wah-wah pedal for electric guitar, introduced in 1967. Credit for popularizing the wah-wah trumpet style probably belongs to Johnny Dunn, a Beale Street musician who left town with W. C. Handy's band and became a leading recording artist of the early 1920s. Dunn's instrumental "Four O'Clock Blues" inspired Robert Johnson's "Four Until Late," the only Johnson lyric that mentions Memphis.

During spring and early summer 1938, the Clyde McCoy "Sugar Blues" Orchestra held a residency at Hotel Claridge, one of the spots Robert reportedly back-doored into to entertain white patrons. McCoy's Claridge gig ended the same night of Robert's final Memphis performance, June 22, 1938.

Mrs. Anderson fondly remembers how much she and her family enjoyed the Palace Theater, one of the vibrant centers of activity on Beale, with its movies, top-flight big-band shows, risqué Midnight Rambles, and the all-important Amateur Night, where many of the city's legendary artists got started.

Anselmo Barrasso owned and operated the Palace. Patrons remember Barrasso's generosity, handing out free hotdogs and admissions to kids during the Depression, so it's easy to imagine Barrasso allowing Johnson to snooze in the theater until the next house party on Short Hernando Street, as Mrs. Anderson recalled.

"It was a beautiful theater, all velvet drapes and gold wallpaper," said Barrasso's wife. "The [chorus line] girls were just gorgeous. They looked just like creamy milk chocolate, they were beautiful girls."

A former news reporter turned history teacher named Nat D. Williams started one of Beale's grand traditions, Amateur Night at the Palace Theater, in which Mrs. Anderson once participated. In February 1937, Dan Burley reported that Amateur Night had run on 102 consecutive Tuesdays, with radio station WNBR broadcasting.

Nat D. also hosted Midnight Rambles, not the sort of entertainment that welcomed children. "The Rambles was really a honky tonk show," said Nat D. "They'd have whiskey, bootleg whiskey. And anything went . . . people would sing vulgar songs, or vulgar dancing. Sometimes women would get out there and almost undress. We'd go over there and drag 'em off."

Across the street from the Palace stood a venerable venue, Pee Wee's Saloon, founded by a man of slight stature but formidable might. The original Pee Wee, Vigelio Maffei, opened the establishment in the 1870s. By 1885, Pee Wee's had become the hangout for local musicians, namely Jim Turner, bandleader and fiddler extraordinaire. Turner taught W. C. Handy "Joe Turner Blues"—a song about Tennessee penal officer Joe Turney—which became the framework of Handy's breakthrough composition, "Memphis Blues." Handy legendarily wrote the song on Pee Wee's cigar counter.

By the time Brother Robert hit Beale Street, Pee Wee had since returned home to Italy, passing the saloon on to a cousin, Lorenzo Pacini. Pee Wee's still welcomed bluesmen, and, after midnight, the pool tables became craps tables.

Directly next door to Pee Wee's stood the photography business of John Henry Evans, a white Pennsylvanian who died in Memphis in 1957, probably unaware of the contribution to history that his coin-operated photo booths had made.

Though Beale served many purposes as an African American community, the street derived its mythical power from intertwined prostitution, gambling, bootlegging, and politics. Mrs. Anderson relates how even her hardworking, God-fearing family were drawn into the local vice world, playing the street lottery known as policy, and patronizing local bootleggers Red Lawrence and Jim Mulcahy.

Robert R. Church, known as the South's first black millionaire, had built his fortune, largely, with brothels. The son of a steamboat captain and an enslaved concubine, Church developed the Memphis red-light district along Gayoso Avenue—one block north of Beale.

In summer 1938, the district ran wide open. An investigator for the American Social Hygiene Association surveyed the scene and left a fascinating record of legalized prostitution, noting, "The traveling man looks upon Memphis as 'a free and easy going city' where persons interested in prostitution may find it without difficulty."

Bellboys and cabbies referred guests to houses and provided johns with an envelope including the resort's name and address, and a code number for the bellboy who made commissions on these referrals.

As the investigator explained, "Each resort has the house number painted in red on the transom over the entrance. At night all shades are drawn, but the interior lights seep out into the pitch-black streets. The music from the automatic phonograph may also be heard along the street . . ."

The red-light district ran so openly due to the green light from local officials. A woman working in one of the houses in 1938 said, "The law is mighty fine in this town. They never bother us at all. They come in, sit around, drink, dance, and even get laid . . ."

Another woman explained the thorough regulation of her trade: "A man don't run no chances when he lays a girl in a house. You see, the law makes us all get examined. No landlady will let a girl hustle until she's been to the doctor. We go twice a month for a smear and once a month for a blood test. If the doctor finds us OK, he sends a report to the city doctor and we can work."

Women posted their health cards in their rooms for customers to inspect. "Believe me, the law comes around, looks at the certificates, and sees that they are right up to date."

Sporting women actively participated in the democratic process. They paid the poll tax—two dollars, same price as a date—and, as one woman explained, "We voted right. The madam told us what to do . . . Hell, I'm from Springfield, Missouri. I don't know one candidate from the other here."

Memphis lingo referred to a woman in the business as a quiff or a chippie, not the doney Robert Johnson sang about in "I Believe I'll Dust My Broom," though Herbert Asbury found that term for prostitute in use in Chicago.

The hygiene society investigator concluded, "For a city of its size Memphis has an unusually large amount of highly commercialized prostitution which constitutes a menace to public health and is provocative to juvenile delinquency."

When the red-light district closed completely in 1940, an expelled prostitute remarked, "It's been going on since the time of Adam and Eve. Well, this is no Garden of Eden. But at that, I'll be lonesome for my room here."

Although the houses of prostitution were tightly regulated in terms of the health and political participation of residents, the places nonetheless served illegal liquor. Tennessee, like other Southern states, kept Prohibition in effect even after the Twenty-First Amendment repealed the national law against alcohol. Bootleggers who made their fortune selling illegal booze were too politically influential to upset.

President's Island, just off the coast of Memphis in the Mississippi River, was where the bootlegging occurred. "They used river water," one distributor recalled. Bluesman

Furry Lewis hauled liquor in the 1920s for famous saloon-keeper Jim Kinnane, whose name is mentioned in recordings by Robert Tim Wilkins and Louise Johnson. Lewis met deliveries from President's Island and brought the liquor to Beale Street. He said, "Boats were running then and Jim sometimes have 50 cases of whiskey where we used to go down to the boat and get it off and bring it up. About five-six of us go there and get it."

The most feared denizen of the Memphis underworld, Red Lawrence, who ran a joint on the street where Robert Johnson stayed with his family, took over the bootlegging racket on Beale in the 1930s.

Musician Alex Sims said, "[Red] had a terrible reputation. He had a place down on Georgia Street."

Violin player Thomas Pinkston, veteran of the Palace Theater orchestra and W. C. Handy's band, recalled, "[Red] only killed about 12 to my knowing. He didn't bother decent people, it was the tramps who didn't have respect for themselves and anyone else and they fool around and get in Red's way, Red would just shoot 'em. That was all and I confidently think he was right for doing it. Now he was nice as he could be, other than don't fool with him or get out of line around him cause he would sure kill you."

At half past two in the morning of February 9, 1937, Red Lawrence shot and killed a man named Eddie Walker who was gambling at his Georgia Avenue establishment. Walker's last words, reportedly, consisted of, "I don't care if you are Red Lawrence."

Walker's death certificate attributes his end to "pistol shot wounds of the head, neck, chest, upper abdomen, and hand."

The homicide occurred two blocks from the Spencer home. Though indicted for murder in the first degree, Red Lawrence walked free just two weeks later when the county grand jury issued a "not true bill" concluding the case.

In addition to Red Lawrence, Mrs. Anderson also remembers bootlegger and political operative Jim Mulcahy. The two men worked together for many years. Mulcahy in particular had a long history with the local civic dictatorship, run by "Boss" E. H. Crump. When Crump had first won election as Memphis mayor in 1909, Mulcahy assisted the campaign.

As dive keeper of the Blue Heaven, Mulcahy needed political protection to operate his bootlegging and gambling joint. He gathered votes for Crump, and volunteered the help of a bandleader who hung around his place, W. C. Handy. The budding composer came up with a campaign tune—"Mr. Crump"—that he later published as "Memphis Blues."

Crump ran the city almost uninterrupted until his death in 1954, and looked out for his supporters—Handy got a park named for him, Mulcahy bootlegged without interference in South Memphis, and Red Lawrence got away with murder.

Mrs. Anderson recalls her brother "Son" hanging around at Red Lawrence's place on Georgia, while Mulcahy still ran a dance hall at the old Blue Heaven site during Robert Johnson's days, less than a mile due east of the Spencer home.

The tall, well-dressed black man who Mrs. Anderson remembers collecting bets for the street lottery known as policy or the numbers worked for a wide-ranging operation under the control of Nello Grandi. Every section of Memphis and every class and race of people played policy compulsively during the 1930s. A convention of gambling syndicates had divided the city into sections, with Grandi controlling the south side, including Beale Street and residential South Memphis, where the Spencers lived.

Grandi had immigrated to the city from Italy, along with a brother, Olento, when neither spoke a word of English. The pair tended bar at Pee Wee's, and witnessed the flourishing gambling business firsthand.

Nello Grandi franchised policy, running the game through hundreds of seemingly innocent neighborhood groceries and cafes that collected bets and held drawings of the winning numbers every day—exactly like the now-legal state lotteries—and extracting a portion of the proceeds.

In 1935, writer Owen White estimated that 500 policy solicitors worked in this city of 200,000 residents.

As a former operator explained, referring to the figure Mrs. Anderson saw around her neighborhood, "The policy writers, when you got a ticket, they'd tell you where the drawing was going to be and what time at what house."

Operators rigged the drawings to limit their losses, but trickle out just enough money to keep players hooked. "Well they would take these balls out was made of ivory and they'd put them in a freezer. They had to have the drawing in front of the people [who played]. And when this guy would stick his hand in the sack to pull a ball out, don't pull one out that was cold, drop it, pull one out that was hot. That's how they used to do that. There was a lot of funny things that happened in them days."

According to Lillie Mae Glover, a Beale Street singer known as Memphis Ma Rainey, legal vice benefitted good behavior. "Let these people gamble," she said. "They could take fifteen, twenty cents and make them some money! Wouldn't have to run around holding up people, understand?"

Pee Wee's always hosted one of the more popular policy games on Beale.

The thrill of old Beale Street died down not long after Robert Johnson's murder in Mississippi in August of 1938. In 1940, at the same time that the red-light district closed, city officials ended quasi-legal gambling. Historian George W. Lee explained, "Gambling places were the nostrils from which Beale Street breathed. And when . . . the lid was tightened down on the gambling places, the color and romance and interest in Beale Street faded. You had two or three nightclubs on Beale Street that kept up some of the interest. You had picture shows and colorful cafes. The hog nose restaurants and chitterling cafes with their pungent odor of barbecue pig and fried fish, remained on

Beale Street, and represented some of the color that once was."

The Palace, Pee Wee's, and Gayoso Avenue are long gone, as are Robert Johnson's Beale Street hangouts that Mrs. Anderson recalls, Church's Park and the One Minute Café. Only Handy Park remains. Thanks to Mrs. Anderson's memories, we know of one more ghost on the Main Street of Black America, and a few of his old haunts.

ACKNOWLEDGMENTS

AA: This book is dedicated to the memory of my daughter Hughia, who believed that my story is just as important as Robert Johnson's. Also to Sister Carrie, who suffered greatly and never got her reward.

I don't know what I would have done without my daughter Sheila, a writer, who helped me edit the manuscript, had our family photograph collection scanned for the book, and who handled communications with Mr. Lauterbach and other people involved with the project. I relied on Sheila throughout the writing of this book and she was always there for me. To note, after doing her homework, she hired Shaun Keough, a young and meticulous Intellectual Property Lawyer with Parker Keough LLP in Newton, Massachusetts. A very special thanks to Mr. Keough.

Special thanks go to my loving family who've helped and supported me all these years, especially my grandsons Eric Anderson and Barry Boyd, and great-grandsons Quintin and Kordell Boyd, who all have strengthened me.

I also want to thank my grandnephew Robert Harris, who is known to the family as the only direct lineage to Brother Robert.

My good friends Jean Jones, Beatrice Todd, Juanita and Leroy Garnett, and Ellen Miller Mack were there for me throughout the years of researching Robert Johnson and attempting to open his estate. Betty Corrigan and Michael Alves were my best blues friends in Boston during the years of my investigative research.

The following institutions at the University of Massachusetts were crucial to my investigative research into opening the Robert Johnson estate: New Africa House, W. E. B. Du Bois Library, and the Blue Wall. I thank their staffs.

Professor Harp and Ed Cohen educated me on the recording of Brother Robert's music. These are very good friends who I'll never forget. Likewise, Dr. Fred Tillis, Archie Shepp, Gilbert McCauley, Emery Smith, Walter Horton, Ed Vaders, Art Steel, Jason Valcourt, Gina Coleman, Ray Copeland, Billy Taylor, Maida Ives, and Avery Sharpe have all lifted my spirit with their music and knowledge. Very special thanks to Matthew Berube, head of information services at Jones Library in Amherst, Massachusetts, and to Jordan Hall, formerly of Amherst Works.

I thank my agent, Paul Bresnick, and editor, Ben Schafer.

PL: This book would not have been possible without John Riley and Maryellen Riley, in memory of George Riley.

It was a pleasure to work with Elijah Wald and Peter Guralnick.

Paul Cartwright shared his research files on a variety of legal and historical aspects of Mrs. Anderson's family history, and I'm grateful to him.

Doug Halijan lent his expertise on an endlessly mysterious issue.

Cheers to Robert Gordon for his kindness, intelligence, creativity, and availability.

Stephanie C. Cosby shared crucial wisdom about the Spencer home site.

Thanks to our many supporters, whose generosity brought Mrs. Anderson and me together to work on this book in Massachusetts and Memphis: Matt Marelius, Robert and Dorothy Pugh, Donna Wooten, Bob Reisman, John Doyle, Chris Carter, Christina McGee, Greil Marcus, Joseph Aaron York, Ted Ownby, Tom Mayer, Scott Barretta, Bill Chapman, Susan May, Lise Yasui, Kevin Cubbins, Eddie Hankins, Brendan Wolfe, Joe Bonomo, Suzanne Henley, Bill Steber, Richard Averitt, Dick Averitt, Adriane Williams, Harvey Bojarsky, Arlo Leach, Christopher Klug, Blake Viar, Steve Tracy, Mark Silliman, Peter Riley, Geffery Stewart, Kristian Odebjer, Steven Davidson, Ann Mintz, Fernando Ortiz de Urbina, Karen Combs, Dan Tappan, Karl Reinsch, Tyler Melton, Deborah Clark, Mike Stillman, Luke Sinden, Tom Ostoyich, Steve Kiviat, Patrik Holmsten, Michael Brosnan,

Acknowledgments

Jan Kotschack, David Suisman, Eli Yamin, Steve Rose, Donal Harris, Nikoo Paydar, Claes Heijbel, and Jean-Michel Dupont.

Thanks finally to editor Ben Schafer, who guided this project, and agent Paul Bresnick, who brought the pieces together.

Index

Page numbers in *italics* indicate photographs or their captions.

Amateur Night and,
  69–70
children of, 10, 17
death of, 91, 92–93
description of, 22–24
at Friendly Lunch
  Room, 45–46
Mama Julia and, 40
wine and, 38–39
Spencer, Theodore
  birth of, 17
  relationship to, 9
Spencer, Willie
  children of, 9
  death of, 17
spirituals, 61
"St. James Infirmary," 61
"St. Louis Blues," 61
St. Paul Avenue, 83, *85*
"Steady Rollin' Man," 130
Steve Miller Band, 126
Stevens, Mr., 112–113
Stokes, Frank, 173
Stonecipher, Norris, 120
"Stones in My Passway," 22
"Sugar Blues," 53, 174
Sumlin, Hubert, 125
Sunnyland Slim, 125
"Sweet Home Chicago," 59,
  61, 84, 125, 158
swimming hole, 72, *72*
switch, railroad, 38, *78*
Sykes, Roosevelt, 125

syphilis, 86

T

Taj Mahal, 126
"Take a Little Walk with
  Me," 58, 158
Tampa Red, 33, 50
"TB Blues," 55
"Tell Me Mama," 126
Temple, Johnny, 33, 46
"Terraplane Blues," 42, 61,
  79, 84, 102, 139,
  158, 160
"That Silver-Haired Daddy
  of Mine," 52, 162
"That's My Man," 68
"This Little Light of Mine,"
  22
Thompson, Caroline Harris
  ("Sister Carrie")
  Annye's errands for,
    49–50
  apartment of, *44*
  caring for Robert
    Johnson, 25–26
  Charles Dodds Spencer
    and, 65
  death of, 134
  description of, 20–22
  Doc Belton and, 83–84
  dress made by, 154
  errands for, 81–82
  gold teeth and, 58